CROSSOVER

CROSSOVER
A VICTORIOUS JOURNEY THROUGH ADVERSITY

TODD HOLTS

Foreword by Juan Martinez

Greatness MAKERS

Crossover © 2023 by Todd Holts. All rights reserved.

Published by Greatness Makers
PO Box 213067, Columbia, SC 29221

www.GreatnessMakers.com

All rights reserved. This book contains material protected under international and federal copyright laws and treaties. Any unauthorized reprint or use of this material is prohibited. No part of this book may be reproduced or transmitted in any form or by any means, electronic or mechanical, including photocopying, recording, or by any information storage and retrieval system, without express written permission from the author.

Identifiers:
LCCN: 2023916422
ISBN: 979-8-9879354-4-6 (paperback)
ISBN: 979-8-9879354-5-3 (ebook)

Available in paperback and e-book.

Edited by Tanya Holts

Scripture quotations from The Authorized (King James) Version. Rights in the Authorized Version in the United Kingdom are vested in the Crown. Reproduced by permission of the Crown's patentee, Cambridge University Press

Scripture quotations marked (NIV) are taken from the Holy Bible, New International Version®, NIV®. Copyright © 1973, 1978, 1984, 2011 by Biblica, Inc.™ Used by permission of Zondervan. All rights reserved worldwide. www.zondervan.com The "NIV" and "New International Version" are trademarks registered in the United States Patent and Trademark Office by Biblica, Inc.™

Any Internet addresses (websites, blogs, etc.) and telephone numbers printed in this book are offered as a resource. They are not intended in any way to be or imply an endorsement by Greatness Makers, nor does Greatness Makers vouch for the content of these sites and numbers for the life of this book.

Contents

FOREWORD — VII
ACKNOWLEDGMENTS — XI
INTRODUCTION — XIII
1. You Will Make It — 1
2. Self-Reflection — 23
3. Righteous Tribulation — 45
4. Divine Transition — 61
5. Intimacy With God — 79
FINAL WORD — 95
About The Author — 99

FOREWORD

Pastor Juan Martinez

BOOKS LIKE THIS ONE are rare gems and very important for the Body of Christ. The very first thing that happened during the fall of man, when they ate the fruit and consumed the lie, was that fear came in. Faith and fear cannot exist together, and we know that "God has not given us a spirit of fear, but of power and of love and of a sound mind" (1 Timothy 1:7). Emotions can be helpful indicators of what is going on in our hearts. Sometimes our emotions are pleasant to experience and sometimes they are not. Sometimes our emotions are grounded in truth, and sometimes emotions are "false" in that they are based upon untrue premises that create destructive behaviors.

Out-of-control emotions tend not to produce God-honoring results. If you want to fix what you do, you must first fix how you think about what you do. A transformed mind comes through spending time with Jesus. If you want to change destructive behaviors and emotions, you must change the heart, which is the way you think!

Whenever I'm going through something, my mentor David Vestal likes to say, "Healthy things grow, growing things change, change brings challenges, and challenges give us the opportunity to trust in God. In other words, every storm, trial, and adversity give you an opportunity to meet GOD.

Pastor Todd has 27 years in ministry and 17 years as a lead Pastor. His wisdom on equipping you to transition through adversity successfully is not just head knowledge but a personal experience he walked out in this book!

I remember meeting Pastor Todd at All Nations School of Ministry. His knowledge of the Bible was a beautiful sight to hear. Yes, you heard that right! I could see what he was saying every time he taught. He had such a passion for the Church to be what Christ intended it to be. He wanted to see the captives free from the lie. He wanted everyone to know that there is one answer to every problem: JESUS! At that moment, I knew I would have a lifelong friend.

Whenever Todd would visit Get Wrapped Church, you could see His love for the Body of Christ. Although at 6 ft 7 in, 325 pounds, he might have looked intimidating but the minute you met him and shook his hand, he would offer the BIGGEST smile. At that moment you knew you were encountering a humble servant of God who was willing to give of his life for another.

He always makes that intentional effort to walk people out of their Egypt. Pastor Todd's book will help you identify the lie so you can accept the truth and become free. When people look at you, they will say, "That's Crazy," and you will say, "NO. That's God!"

I pray that as you read this book you will allow it to renew your mind, and that you will get a passion and heart to develop an intimate relationship with our Lord and savior, Jesus Christ. You were created as a victor, not a victim. Your citizenship is in

Heaven. You belong to a Body of Christ known as Heavicans with a King named Jesus. As His ambassadors, we are called to the ministry of reconciliation and to set the captives free.

-Juan Martinez, Senior Pastor,
Get Wrapped Church, Spring, Texas

ACKNOWLEDGMENTS

There are countless people that I desire to thank for your love and support of me in both life and ministry.

First, to my wife, Tanya. Without question, you are my greatest earthly passion and treasure. I am in awe of the treasure God entrusted to me when He gave me you. Thank you for your unfailing love, your unwavering faithfulness, your continued encouragement, and your enduring friendship. I love you more than words can express. Thank you for allowing me the privilege of doing life with you.

To my children - Tyrah, Tohnnia, and Christian. The three of you are the most incredible gifts for which any father could ask. It has been so amazing to experience life with you. Know that I am extremely proud of who you have become. I love you more than words can express. Continue trusting God and pushing towards your dreams. Daddy loves you!

To Pastors Juan and Ruthy Martinez, in a season of unexpected transition, Tanya and I are truly grateful to have the two of you as pastors, mentors and, most of all friends. It is our tremendous honor to do life with you both.

To Get Wrapped Church, thank you for being the spiritual pillow on which God has allowed me and my family to rest and heal. I am eternally grateful to God for providing us with a community of faith that consistently displays Christ's unconditional love in the way you do. I am truly honored to *"hangout"* with all of you.

From the bottom of my heart, Thank you!

INTRODUCTION

My Usable Testimony

Revelations 12:10-11 NIV
10 Then I heard a loud voice in heaven say: "Now have come the salvation and the power and the kingdom of our God, and the authority of His Messiah. For the accuser of our brothers and sisters, who accuses them before our God day and night, has been hurled down. 11 They triumphed over him by the blood of the Lamb and <u>by the word of their testimony</u>...

AS TESTIMONIES GO, I guess you could say I have a pretty good one. At one time in my life, I found myself divorced, homeless, running from the calling of God on my life, over eight hundred miles from home, and too ashamed to go back due to fear of what people would think of me. Then God, graciously and supernaturally, grabbed me and restored my life with a new ministry, a new marriage, and a new hope.

Now this being said, you would think I would be fully confident in sharing my story with others, yet doing so has always been a challenge for me. Despite all God has brought me through in life, I have always questioned if I had anything to offer or say to others. When I first felt like God was leading me to write this book, I procrastinated for a long time thinking that no one would be interested in what I had to say. For whatever reason, I figured no one would want to hear from a person who had failed as much as I had. I was a failure in ministry, as well as a failure in marriage. I was uneducated with an unfulfilling job. I struggled with a roller coaster of emotional brokenness and self-esteem issues. What wisdom could I possibly have to offer?

One day in my prayer time while preparing for a sermon, God said four words to me that changed my mind concerning sharing my testimony and giving this "book thing" a try. He said, *"It's not about you."* Four simple words, holding such profound meaning that they continue to provide the framework for how I view every part of my life.

In that very moment, God shared with me that true success in every area of life would have very little to do with me and everything to do with Him. It was not that I wouldn't have to put in work. Obedience and faithfulness are always necessary components of success, but even in work, true success has never been, nor ever will be, possible apart from Him. Just as the seeds that a farmer plants cannot produce a harvest without God sending the rain, neither will any area of life prosper apart from God's grace and anointing.

> John 1:1-3 NIV
> 1 In the beginning was the Word, and the Word was with God, and the Word was God. 2 He was with God in the beginning. 3 Through Him all things were made; without Him nothing was made that has been made.

Jesus is God's Anointed One. Because of Him, all things have been made and all things have found their being. Through Him everything will continue to be made and continue to be sustained. In line with this truth, it is not my anointing that will cause this book to be successful. It is His anointing working through me. I am only responsible for my part. I must be obedient to what I have been commanded to do and the rest is up to Him. One of the greatest revelations I have ever come to in life is this: God is not interested in what we can do for Him. He is only interested in what we will allow Him to do through us, in His strength. Success or failure is *"not about me."* Whatever the outcome, it is all about Him, through Him.

John 9 gives the account of a man who was seemingly so insignificant that his name was never mentioned. The only description of the man was that he had been blind from birth. It's amazing to me how people often define others by their faults, failures, and limitations as if where they are now is where they will always be. However, Jesus did not define this man by his limitations. Jesus defined him by His own limitless power to do something miraculous in his life. After being healed by Jesus, this man gave the most simple yet, at the same time, one of the most profound testimonies concerning his experience with Jesus. *"One thing I know; whereas I was once blind, now I see."* This is a testimony that rings just as loud today as it did then. God regularly uses authentic testimony to reveal His divine nature. No matter how insignificant they are thought to be, testimonies are the vehicles God uses to bring Himself glory.

The Bible warns us to *"know the schemes of the enemy."* Attacking the confidence of personal testimonies is Satan's go-to tactic because it accomplishes two things:

1. Attacking the confidence of testimony reduces the faith-influence believers have amongst one another. One of the primary ways faith is developed in people is through impartation. Impartation is the supernatural transference of faith from one person to another through life experience. *"Faith comes by hearing, and hearing by the word of God (Romans 10:17)."* If the enemy can get you to close your mouth concerning the great things God has done for you, by default, he can limit faith in others due to their lack of exposure to what God can do supernaturally. Sharing testimony provides tangible context in which other believers develop reasonable hope and expectation for God to show up in their lives in a similar way. When others see what God has done in your life, their faith will begin to grow for Him to do the same in theirs.

2. Attacking the confidence of testimony also hinders the advancement of the divine purpose of God to evangelize the unsaved world. Just as God uses testimony to impart faith for supernatural expectations amongst believers, He also utilizes testimony as entry points of faith for those who are not yet saved. Personal testimony is the primary method God employs to reveal Himself to a dying world and to reconcile that world to Himself. Romans 10:14 asks the question, *"How will they hear without a preacher?"* The word *preacher* in this text is the Greek word *kēryssō*, which means *one who publishes or proclaims openly something that has been done.* Sharing the character of God and compelling unbelievers to come to God is not something to be limited to ordained clergy. Your testimony and proclamation of God's goodness is just as important in God's plan to evangelize the world.

As unimportant as I have sometimes reasoned my testimony to be, today I am trusting that God can and will use it to plant His Gospel of love in your heart. I am also believing that God will anoint it to grow you in maturity concerning His purpose and plan for your life.

Sharing my testimony reminds me of the story of a Hebrew mother, Jochebed, and her infant child, Moses. In fear for her son's life, Moses' mother constructed a small ark, waterproofed it, put him inside, and then placed it amongst the reeds along the banks of the Nile River. Right away, you are able to see the faith of Moses' mother. The dangers that live amongst riverbanks in this region of the world are numerous. There are snakes, crocodiles, extreme temperatures, and so many other things that could have caused harm to her son. It is very clear that the hand of God was with Moses from the beginning. His mother went to great lengths to make the ark as secure as she possibly could. However, her hands were not the hands ultimately responsible for his survival. All she could do was obey what God told her and leave the rest up to Him. In the end, it would be God who would deliver Moses into his divine destiny. God would be the cause, so only God could get the glory.

In the same way, I offer the wisdom from my life while trusting God. As it sits in the reeds of your hands, by faith, I believe that God will use my efforts to bring about a breakthrough for you. If you find that you are blessed by anything you receive, please give all praise and credit to God to whom it is due. All that I do is for Him, through Him, and because of Him.

As I stated earlier, faith is the result of a person hearing God's Word. My prayer is that *Crossover* will be a tool that God graces to reveal His Word and to boost your faith moving forward. I pray it encourages you to win in adverse circumstances. In *Crossover*, you will receive wisdom gleaned during my personal times of difficulty. Within its pages, you will find instructional nuggets extracted from challenging life moments. This labor of love is purposed to encourage and strengthen you to cross over into a victorious life.

> 2 Timothy 3:16-17 NIV
> 16 All Scripture is God-breathed and is useful for teaching, rebuking, correcting, and training in righteousness, 17 so that the servant of God may be thoroughly equipped for every good work.

The foundation of all that is offered in *Crossover* is fully based on Biblical Scripture. I encourage you to go back and study every thought very carefully. Test every point by God's Word. The more you personally study and understand, the better equipped you will become to crossover into your God-ordained destiny.

I hope that you are overflowing with faith and expectation concerning what God is about to do on your behalf. BE EXCITED! BE VERY EXCITED! Even if you are not, know that I am super excited for you! This is truly a divine moment of destiny. As an ancient proverb states, *"A journey of a thousand miles begins with a single step."* So it is with you today. Most people who find themselves in negative circumstances never really seek a way out. They just learn to adjust and deal with it. In doing so, they go through life accepting a substandard existence because they feel that it is the only choice they have. They have been ordained by God to be overcomers, yet they have settled for dysfunction and pain. Not you! You have decided today, by reading this book, that there has to be something better for you than where you are right now. You have committed to taking the steps necessary to change your future by seeking God's wisdom today. Good for you! Know that I am super proud of you. Stay encouraged! There is light at the end of the tunnel. You will make it! You will Crossover!

CHAPTER 1

You Will Make It

MATTHEW 10:41 TELLS US that anyone who receives a prophet also receives the *"prophet's reward."* The prophet's reward talked about in this passage is the actual manifestation of the prophecy that has been spoken by the prophet. Whenever a true prophetic word goes forth, an individual's ability to receive the word spoken over them will be the direct result of the person believing and then acting on the word they received. With this in mind, allow me to prophesy over you: *YOU WILL MAKE IT! The situation you are facing will not get the best of you. You will come out of this on top. In Jesus' name, Amen!*

Oftentimes, when you're going through something you can feel so overwhelmed and stressed out that you want to give up. Everything seems to be against you, and you see no way out. You feel like the fox that is being hunted by a pack of bloodhounds. All you hear is the bark of the enemy, as circumstances become more and more difficult to navigate. With anxiety rising, causing your impending doom to feel closer and closer, you begin to see yourself becoming the trophy on the Devil's wall. However, it is important for you to know that even in times when you can't see your way, God always has a way of escape available to you that is closer than you think.

> 1 Corinthians 10:13 KJV
>
> 13 There hath no temptation taken you, but such as is common to man: but God is faithful, who will not suffer you to be tempted above that ye are able; but will with the temptation also make a way to escape, that ye may be able to bear it.

Because of the faithfulness of God, know with certainty that with every temptation there is an ordained doorway of freedom available to you. God will not leave you hanging. Not only does He have a way out for you, but the way out is one that allows you to win while at the same time maintaining Godly character. The challenge for you is not to give up before you find the door He has provided.

Though you may not be able to see it right now, the first thing you have to tell yourself is, *"God has a door for me somewhere."* Purpose to focus on the possibility of becoming victorious over adversity rather than focusing on the possibility of continued struggle. Learn to envision yourself winning rather than failing. The obstacle for most people is that they tend to focus more on the problems that they face instead of the opportunities that problems offer them. True, your situation appears bleak. The natural facts of your condition do not appear to be changing. However, focusing on the possibility of failure will not make your situation any better. Focusing on failure will only cause you to gravitate toward that reality. Job said it this way, *"What I have feared has come upon me; what I dreaded has happened to me (Job 3:25 NIV)."* Proverbs 23:7 teaches us that our present thought patterns are the birthplace of our future circumstances.

Our meditations and belief systems are the seeds of tomorrow's realities.

> Our meditations and belief systems are the seeds of tomorrow's realities. Whenever you allow fear to govern your perspective about what you are going through, you give the devil the legal right to manifest negative circumstances in your life.

Whenever you allow fear to govern your perspective about what you are going through, you give the devil the legal right to manifest negative circumstances in your life. Because adversity is a part of every person's experience, it is critical that you develop the capacity to trust God for open doors despite adversities.

Jesus said in John 16.33, *"In this life you shall have tribulation: but be of good cheer; I have overcome the world."* Adversity is unavoidable. It is the product of the fallen state of humanity. Through one man, Adam, sin and its adverse effects became forever bound to the human experience. However, even in the face of adversity, Jesus commands us to be of good cheer. In other words, just because your circumstances may be unfavorable or unpleasant, it doesn't mean that your perspective has to be. Determine to shift your attention from the difficulty of what you're going through, to the faithfulness of The ONE who has promised to bring you through it. Learn to rejoice in the fact that in Christ there are unlimited possibilities in the midst of problems. Never allow tough times to cloud your faith to the open doors that you have in Jesus Christ. Even when you have no physical strength left, don't give up on the prospects you have in Christ. God can and will perfect His power in your circumstances, even when you want to give up. No matter how bad your situation gets, hold on to the supernatural possibilities that a life in Christ affords.

God of Limitless Possibilities

> Colossians 1:16-17 NIV
> 16 For in Him all things were created: things in heaven and on earth, visible and invisible, whether thrones or powers or rulers or authorities; all things have been created through Him and for Him. 17 He is before all things, and in Him all things hold together.

In December 1995, I found myself in my mid-twenties, unemployed, living at home with my parents. In the midst of an extremely rocky relationship with my natural father, one day after coming home, a pretty scary argument broke out between the two of us. With the exchange of threats and emotions at a boil, I knew that my time of living at home had come to an end. With this revelation, I decided to load all I had into my car and get as far away from the tall pines of Lamar County Georgia as I could. With nothing more than a tank of gas and forty-five dollars to my name, I set out on a journey that would change my life forever.

Because of a childhood friend I knew who was living in Port Arthur, Texas, I decided that would be my destination. Before leaving, while looking over my car to make sure that it was okay for the drive, I noticed my tires were so badly worn that wire was visible in the tread of two of them. Seeing their condition, questions began to circle in my mind concerning the sensibility of this trip. It was very apparent to me that if anything unfortunate happened before arriving at my destination (i.e., flat tire) it would prove to be incredibly problematic based on my lack of resources. Nevertheless, armed with a saying that I often heard my mother use, *"God protects babies and fools,"* I started on my journey anyway. Little did I know how rough the highways between Georgia and Texas were. With every pothole I hit, I grew increasingly afraid that the next bump would surely take me out. Full of anxiety, I continued to have this haunting image of myself with flat tires, stranded on some dark stretch of road, miles away from any semblance of assistance. Yet, despite my fears, and the bumps that continued to come, those tires held up all the way. Fourteen hours and eight hundred miles later, I arrived in Port Arthur, Texas safe and sound.

Now this event may not seem like much to you, but every time I think back on this drive, I am amazed at the undeniable truth it portrays concerning God's character. No matter how impossible or improbable things may appear, when purposed by God, He has the uncanny ability to do what seemingly can't be done. There's no way those tires should've held up in the shape they were in, but God is faithful. Not only did my tires stay together for a trip spanning half the country, they also lasted for another two months of driving after arriving in Texas. The point of the story is this, *"What is impossible with man is possible with God (Luke 18:27)."* Even when you feel worn down and about to break, God can and will sustain you. In the roughest of times, He is more than capable of holding things together until you reach your destination. Though there may be a few bumps and potholes along the way, you can trust that God will never leave you nor forsake you. According to Psalm 138:8, God is more than capable of perfecting those things that are concerning you. You only need to believe that He will and trust Him to do so.

To trust God, you're going to have to release Him from the limitations of your natural mind. Most of us place human limitations on a limitless God. We try to confine God to the boundaries of what we understand, even though that understanding is flawed and incomplete at best. We take the position that God is incapable of doing something in our lives because of our inability to explain how He could do it. We dumb God down to the level of human inadequacies and limitations, although neither human ignorance or earthly limitations have any bearing on God's ability, authority, and power to move. God does not need man's validation to be who He is. He is fully sovereign, fully self-sustained, and fully unmoved by man's opinions of Him. Man's inability to understand something does not limit God's abilities or faithfulness. There are no limitations or inadequacies in God. Even when we can't logically explain how He can do something, it does not change the reality that He still can. Here is a thought for you. We say that we want God to grant us a peace that surpasses all understanding; yet we always kick, scream, and cry when He requires that we trust Him without the understanding that we desire.

> God does not need man's validation to be who He is. He is fully sovereign, fully self-sustained, and fully unmoved by man's opinions of Him.

This is why Galatians 3:11 states, *"...the righteous live by faith."* God expects you to live past the boundaries of your natural understanding. Most Christians put more faith in man-made things than they do in God's abilities. Think about it. Do you know exactly how your refrigerator works? Do you know the mechanical ins and outs of how your automobile works? I don't know about you, but I don't. There are a lot of things that I rely on in life that I cannot explain the details of how they work, yet that does not stop me from trusting them to work. I simply choose to trust in them past my limited understanding. I don't have to know how they work to trust that they will work when I use them. Having faith is not believing God because you have all the answers. Having faith is the ability to trust God in the absence of answers. To take it a step further, faith is moving forward when the only answer you have is God. God's ways are higher than our ways, and His thoughts are higher than our thoughts. You have to realize that no matter how much you learn about God, you will always be challenged to trust Him past what you are able to naturally understand.

When I was writing the first edition of this book my son, Christian, was only three years old. At that age, he had begun to explore and get into everything humanly possible for a person his size. Throughout this exploration process, it was amazing to see him learn and navigate new experiences from day to day. However, despite his tremendous capacity to pick up various skills and information, there were still many things he encountered that he was unable to do on his own. Subsequently, every time he faced something above his ability to understand or do himself, his default response would be to run to his mother and me to do it for him. Although he didn't have a clue how either of us would accomplish the task, he would simply trust that we could and believed that we would. In the same way, life will take you through circumstances that require a willingness for you to trust your Heavenly Father to do things that are beyond your natural understanding of how He can.

>Proverbs 4:7 KJV
>7 Wisdom is the principal thing; therefore, get wisdom and with all thy getting get understanding.

Make the decision today to trust God past your normal capacity to comprehend. A walk of faith that pleases God sometimes requires obedience, even in moments when you don't have all the information that your flesh desires. Proverbs 4 states that *"Wisdom is the principal thing..."* The word principal here means *"the first or most important."* Please be aware that wisdom and understanding are not the same. Wisdom is the ability to follow divine instruction. Understanding is the ability to comprehend those instructions. Faith moments are not birthed out of what you understand, but they are birthed out of your immovable trust in God, in the face of your lack of understanding. Faith is the act of moving forward, even when you don't know.

Having the ability to please God by faith means that there will always be times when wisdom and obedience are required, apart from your adequate insight on how, when, or why. I am sure Abraham would have loved to have known where God was sending him when He said, *"Go to a place that I will show you."* But, if Abraham had possessed all the facts concerning his journey, then it would not have been a walk of faith. GOING is often the faith requirement that releases God's SHOWING.

In Genesis 6, Noah is commanded by God to build an ark for himself, his family, and all the animals to save them from the flood. To understand the faith that Noah was required to walk in, you must first understand that it had never rained on the earth before this point in time. To build an ark in anticipation of rain which he had never witnessed meant that Noah would have to operate in wisdom apart from prior personal experience. Noah was forced to ignore everything he understood to be true and walk in the wisdom of God's divine instruction. His ability to do so ultimately made all the difference in the deliverance of his family from the flood. Though understanding should always be the ultimate objective, many times the doorway to understanding tomorrow is the choice to walk in wisdom today. Romans 9:33 says *"The one who trusts in the Lord will never be put to shame."* Whenever you trust God past your understanding, you can be assured that understanding will soon follow. We have this assurance in God based on His covenant promise to watch over His Word to see that it is performed.

When the rain stopped and the flood waters decreased on the earth, the ark Noah built came to rest on the majestic peaks of Mount Ararat. This extraordinary image provides a prophetic reminder of God's faithfulness towards His children when they choose to simply trust and obey Him. Proverbs 3:5 admonishes believers to trust in God over their personal understanding. When you do so, God supernaturally directs your steps towards His best for your life. Your consistency in choosing to trust and obey God, independent of your understanding and experience, will always elevate you to greater levels of divine grace. With every submission of your personal will to God, you can expect your life to come to rest atop greater plateaus of intimacy, wisdom, authority, vision, provision, and much more.

So be encouraged within your circumstances. You serve a God of limitless possibilities. No matter what, God can and will see you through. Your impossibilities are only opportunities for God to reveal Himself as the awesome Father that He is. Your season of difficulty is a prime opportunity for God to shower you with His limitless love. Ponder these thoughts for a second. You serve a God who speaks worlds into existence. You serve a God who makes the winds stand at attention with just a thought. You serve a God who causes blind men to see and dead men to rise to life again. So why would He have any problem delivering you from any level of adversity? You only need to hold onto your faith in God and to the limitless possibilities you have in trusting Him.

Expecting The Goodness of God

> Psalm 27:13 NIV
> I remain confident of this: I will see the goodness of the LORD in the land of the living.

One secret to overcoming negative circumstances is learning how to maintain an enduring expectation of God's goodness manifesting in your life. It is your spiritual right to overcome problems with total victory. Possessing an enduring expectation should never be based on morality or right behavior. An enduring expectation is a spiritual right that you possess, by faith, in the finished work of Christ's sacrifice at Calvary. Romans 8:17 refers to believers as *"joint heirs"* with Christ. This means that everything Jesus inherited, through His death and resurrection from the dead, also belongs to you. From Ephesians 1:20-21 we understand that Jesus has been raised to the right hand of God *"...far above every principality, power, might, dominion, and name ... throughout the ages."* In Ephesians 2:6 we find that this same position, power, might, and dominion are also available to those who choose to live in obedience to His Lordship. Because of your faith in this promise, you should expect and can expect to win in every situation. In reality, the circumstance that is opposing you has already been defeated through Jesus' triumph over death. You only need to hold fast and stay the course of faith until circumstances manifest in your favor.

Because all principalities and powers are under your feet through your faith in Jesus Christ, you also possess the spiritual right to expect demonic spirits and opposition to obey you. In the same way police officers anticipate that citizens will comply with their commands, you should expect the same where the enemy is concerned. People don't respond to the orders of police simply due to who they are as natural men and women. People submit to police due to the authority of the government that backs them and the weapons that they carry on their sides. Similarly, darkness yields to the authority of believers because of the power of the Kingdom they represent and the Word they carry in their hearts.

As battlelines were drawn between the Philistine army and the armies of Israel in 1 Samuel 17, David makes a powerful statement to Goliath that illustrates the authority believers possess in Christ.

> 1 Samuel 17:45-46 NIV
> 45 David said to the Philistine, "You come against me with sword and spear and javelin, but I come against you in the name of the Lord Almighty, the God of the armies of Israel, whom you have defied. 46 This day the Lord will deliver you into my hands, and I'll strike you down and cut off your head. This very day I will give the carcasses of the Philistine army to the birds and the wild animals, and the whole world will know that there is a God in Israel.

David's confidence in his ability to defeat Goliath had nothing to do with his faith in his own abilities and strength. His confidence emanated from his faith in God. David knew his tactical advantage was beyond his physical skillset. His power rested in his supernatural relationship and unwavering faith in God. The justification for every expectation you have should always originate from your total faith in who God is, not in who you are. By natural standards, David possessed neither the size, strength, experience, nor weaponry to defeat a soldier as skilled as Goliath. However, what he did have was an overwhelming confidence in the power and faithfulness of Jehovah, who would fight the battle for him. David expected to win against Goliath because David knew the fight was bigger than him. He understood that Goliath's defiance was more spiritual than physical. Goliath didn't know anything about David prior to this encounter. So, Goliath was not opposing David. Goliath was opposing God. Whenever you face adversity in life, it is more often about the Devil attempting to oppose God's glory than it is about him opposing you as a person. Therefore, when you openly acknowledge Jesus as Lord and strive to live according to His will, you can confidently expect to triumph in every situation. Whenever you put your faith in God, He becomes obligated to defend His name, His power, and His authority, which you represent. When you win, God wins. In every adversity continue to tell yourself *"This fight is bigger than me."* Face every difficulty with the confidence that God will cause you to triumph in every situation for His name's sake. The battle is not yours. It belongs to the LORD. You are only His representative sent to witness and document how He wins the battle. Expect to win!

1 Samuel 17:48 NIV
48 As the Philistine moved closer to attack him, David ran quickly toward the battle line to meet him.

Expectation is not merely a thought; it is an action. Expectation involves an outward expression of one's readiness concerning a thought, belief, or desire. It is a forward movement of faith to position yourself to receive what you say you are believing God for.

When my wife and I were expecting our son, Christian, we began to make preparations for his arrival months in advance. Furniture was purchased. Bottles, clothes, and diapers were stocked. A room was painted, and multiple doctor's visits were attended in expectation of the bundle of joy that would soon grace our presence. Our beliefs caused us to take actions that corresponded with the baby boy that we were expecting.

The truest sign of expectation will always be a forward movement that positions you closer to the reality that you are believing for. What actions are you making that prove your expectation of God's goodness in your life? What works have you partnered with your expectations to activate your anticipated breakthrough? As previously stated, what *GOING* are you displaying in anticipation of God's *SHOWING*?

> The truest sign of expectation will always be a forward movement that positions you closer to the reality that you are believing for.

If you are expecting to be debt-free someday, what stewardship principles are you putting in place concerning your finances? If you are expecting to lose weight, what dietary changes are you making and what kind of exercise plan have you put in place to facilitate your desired weight loss? Don't be passive about your deliverance. Don't be complacent concerning the battle before you. Prepare for it! Pursue it! Possess it! Understand the authority you have in God. Seek His wisdom and develop a plan. Then take the fight to the Devil with the full expectation of being victorious. David fully expected to defeat Goliath. In turn, he paired his actions with his beliefs by preparing and pursuing the opportunity to fight.

One disturbing statement people often approach me with is, *"Pastor, please pray for me. The Devil is really attacking me today."* Now, I do understand and sympathize with the struggles many are going through, but I wonder why I never seem to get as many requests related to the other side of the coin? Why don't I ever have people say, *"Pastor, please pray for me today! I'm going on a full-scale assault of the enemy, and I am believing to win in a big way!"* True expectation is not uninspired or timid, it attacks.

David's expectation can be fully seen in how he spoke to, and in how he attacked, Goliath. If a person truly expects to win, it will always be visible in both words and actions. Be a person of expectation and begin to assault, with assurance, what seeks to destroy you.

Maintaining A Winning Mindset

> Proverbs 23:7a KJV
> 7 For as he thinks in his heart, so is he.

Your mind is the doorway by which the spirit realm manifests itself in your natural life. Your thoughts are the birth canal of your future realities. Spirits do not have the legal right to manifest in the earth realm without agreement from a physical body. Your thoughts, beliefs, and behavior are entry points by which spirits gain access into the natural realm. In Genesis 1, God has given mankind full authority, dominion, and stewardship of the earth. Whether Godly or demonic, the spiritual realm cannot enter the physical realm without first having agreement from flesh of some kind. This is important because it gives us insight into how destinies are shaped. Your destiny will ultimately be determined by the thought patterns with which you choose to agree. Bringing your thoughts into alignment with the mind of God is critical to your overcoming and even preventing negative circumstances in the future. You not only have to expect to win, but you must also make that expectation of winning the genesis of every related internal belief and every external action. No matter what the situation, you should always maintain thinking consistent with the truth of God's Word. This is the foundation of developing a winning mindset.

> 2 Corinthians 10:3-5 NIV
> 3 For though we walk in the flesh, we do not war after the flesh: 4 For the weapons of our warfare are not carnal, but mighty through God to the pulling down of strongholds; 5 Casting down imaginations, and every high thing that exalts itself against the knowledge of God and bringing into captivity every thought to the obedience of Christ.

One challenge to maintaining a winning mindset is possessing a clear understanding of the difference between natural facts and eternal truth. Many believers struggle in life because they typically hold facts in higher regard than they do truth, but truth is vastly superior. Natural facts are physical estimations of what can be seen. They are the perceptions of what is taking place in life through the calculation of man's five senses. Facts are man's limited view of what is happening around them without regard to the existence and involvement of a supernatural God. Truth is God's eternal perspective. It is the testimony of Jesus. Truth is natural facts viewed intentionally through the lens of God's divine involvement. Truth is God's written Word, and it is God's perspective void of fear or carnal influence. Truth is the intentional acceptance and active application of God's divine perspective that has been revealed through Biblical Scripture.

The winning mindset draws its confidence in the revealed nature and character of God. Because Jesus is the same yesterday, today, and forever, the winning mindset gains stability in knowing that the victorious God that has always been is the victorious God that will always be. Throughout the scope of scripture, we are shown the nature of God to be both omnipresent and sovereign. Omnipresence refers to God's divine nature to always exist in all places at all times. He not only exists in all places on a particular day in time, He exists in every dimension of time, in every season of time, in every period of time, all at the same time. Thus, God is in every place in the present. He is in every place and dimension of our past, and He is in every place and dimension of our future. Where you have come from, God is. Where you are, God is. Where you are going, God is already there.

Sovereignty speaks to God's unequaled supremacy in every place and dimension where He exists. There is no moment in time when God has not held full authority and power. There is no season of existence when He has had to bow His knee. As such, there will never be a time in the future when God will be subject to anyone or anything. It is from this perspective that we gain strength for a winning mindset. When thoughts of failure arise, the winning mindset rejects natural facts and finds hope in God's omnipresence and complete sovereignty. A winning mindset demands that you practice the discipline of holding eternal truth above natural facts. Based on a working understanding of God's divine nature and character, a winning mindset believes and expects to come out victorious. Regarding truth over facts does not mean that you ignore the reality of natural facts.

To do this would be irresponsible. Regarding truth over facts means that you choose to operate with the understanding that natural facts do not change the supremacy of God's truth, nor do they change His character. God's character and abilities are not diminished in the face of facts. They are actually revealed.

> Regarding truth over facts means that you choose to operate with the understanding that natural facts do not change the supremacy of God's truth, nor do they change His character.

Romans 4:18-21 NIV
18 Against all hope, Abraham in hope believed and so became the father of many nations, just as it had been said to him, "So shall your offspring be." 19 Without weakening in his faith, he faced the fact that his body was as good as dead—since he was about a hundred years old—and that Sarah's womb was also dead. 20 Yet he did not waver through unbelief regarding the promise of God but was strengthened in his faith and gave glory to God, 21 being fully persuaded that God had power to do what he had promised.

The facts of Abraham's natural condition were directly opposed to God's promise for his life. However, Abraham chose to regard God's promise above what natural facts suggested. Though Abraham recognized that his body was as good as dead, he still determined to have faith in God. Against the existence of natural facts, he remained consistent in behavior that reflected his unwavering faith in what God told him he would become. Prioritizing truth over natural facts is a skill that you, as a believer, must purpose to mature in. Until you learn to resist thinking that is contrary to divine truth, you will continue to find yourself controlled by demonic influences and living life far below the standard God has for you.

In Matthew 4, we see Jesus' mastery of this skill as we witness His conversation with Satan in the wilderness during the onset of His public ministry. When looking at this passage, it is important that you understand what is really taking place. Contrary to the picture that many conjure in their minds, these verses do not show a conversation between Jesus and a physical devil, carrying a pitchfork, in a red onesie, with horns. These verses show Jesus facing the enemy in much the same way that we do daily. They show Jesus being attacked in His mind. Satan attempted to get Jesus to accept lies and thoughts that were contrary to the truth of God's Word. When Satan urged Jesus to turn rocks into bread, He was dealing with the same spirit of carnality that tries to persuade believers to acquire things outside of God's divine order. When Jesus is challenged to cast Himself off a cliff to see if angels would rescue Him, Jesus was dealing with a suicidal spirit, attempting to get Him to take His life before He fulfilled His God given purpose and destiny. When Jesus was offered the riches of this world in exchange for His worship, He was dealing with a spirit of greed and materialism that sacrifices godly character, morals, and a personal relationship with God for worldly prosperity and fame.

With each attempt by the enemy to corrupt His thinking, Jesus immediately responded with the truth of God's Word. With every attack, Jesus responded with *"It is written..."* Once the enemy saw that he could not get Jesus to accept his lies, scripture declares that Satan gave up and left Him. The revelation is, as you begin to consistently ground your thoughts and actions in God's truth, you will begin to see the enemy flee from you more and more.

> James 1:4-8 KJV
> 4 But let patience have her perfect work, that ye may be perfect and entire, wanting nothing. 5 If any of you lack wisdom, let him ask of God, that giveth to all men liberally and without reproach; and it shall be given him. 6 But let him ask in faith, nothing wavering. For he that wavereth is like a wave of the sea driven with the wind and tossed. 7 For let not that man think that he shall receive any thing of the Lord. 8 A double minded man is unstable in all his ways.

The stability of every person's life is a direct result of their thoughts. Whenever you are unstable in what you consistently think (double-minded), you can expect your life to manifest dysfunction, disorder, and discomfort. James warns that anyone who struggles with inconsistent thoughts should not expect God to do anything for them. However, the man who has learned to control his thoughts and remain stabilized in God's eternal wisdom can also expect to be anchored in a supernatural flow of holistic blessings and increase.

Now it is important to understand that the mind of God is not automatically pre-wired in a person. It has to be desired and pursued. Matthew 7:7 says, *"Ask, and it shall be given unto you; seek, and ye shall find; knock, and the door shall be open unto you."* God is gentle in nature. He will never force anything on you that you don't desire to have. Consequently, He has made this individual longing a prerequisite of possessing His mind and wisdom. It is a part of the nature of free will.

> Colossians 1:9-11a KJV
> 9 For this cause we also, since the day we heard it, do not cease to pray for you, and to desire that ye might be filled with the knowledge of His will in all wisdom and spiritual understanding; 10 That ye might walk worthy of the Lord unto all pleasing, being fruitful in every good work, and increasing in the knowledge of God; 11 Strengthened with all might, according to His glorious power.

When you earnestly desire to make the thoughts of God your thoughts, His Spirit makes wisdom available to you without hindrance. As you hunger, God freely opens the door of His heart to you, so that you possess the ability to *"be filled with the knowledge of His will in all wisdom and spiritual understanding..."* By aligning your thoughts with His divine wisdom and understanding, you are then empowered to *"walk worthy of the Lord, fully pleasing unto Him, being fruitful in every good work and increasing in His knowledge, strengthened with all might, according to His glorious power..."*

Psalm 42:1-2 NIV
1 As the deer pants for streams of water, so my soul pants for You, my God. 2 My soul thirsts for God, for the living God. When can I go and meet with God?

Desiring the mind of God is also not just a thought or a feeling. It is an intentional action. Deer instinctively migrate to water because it is their epicenter of life. Vegetation thrives around lakes, ponds, and streams. Therefore, water sources become the pursuit of deer because of the valued life components they provide. Similarly, believers are called to pursue the mind of God as their life source. Believers thrive when they willingly submit to God's wisdom. *"In Him we live and move and have our being (Acts 17:28 NIV)."* Hebrews 11:6 tells us that God is *"a rewarder of them that diligently seek Him."*

As you diligently pursue God's mind through His written Word, your thinking becomes renewed, your intentions become transformed, and your destiny draws closer to His divine purpose. Developing a winning mindset is a commitment to transforming the way you think to how God thinks. It is the diligent process of tearing down old, contrary ideologies and replacing them with God's eternal truth revealed through scripture. Much like renewing your physical body, developing a winning mindset takes a consistent, daily regimen of diet and exercise. The more disciplined you are at feeding yourself the Word of God and exercising its principles, the more effective you will become in overcoming adverse circumstances in your life.

CHAPTER 2

Self-Reflection

"I'm sorry, Mr. Holts. We cannot extend you any more time. Unless you are able to come up with the full payment today, we will be forced to come and pick up the car."

During the winter of 1996, I experienced the embarrassment of having a car repossessed. The same car God once held the tires together on while driving to Texas was now being taken away from me because of my failure to make the required payments. The first big purchase of my life was now becoming an enduring scar on my credit report. After it was repossessed, for years I was unable to make any major purchases due to my extremely poor credit rating. Throughout the years, I continued to blame everybody else for my struggles and never took responsibility for my shortcomings. Why couldn't anyone see that I was trustworthy? Many times, I would even try to rationalize my credit struggles with the spiritual position, the Devil was trying to keep me from having what God had planned for me, as if that is even possible for him to do. Or, I would say that God must have something better for me if He was not allowing my approval to go through. Over time, I matured enough to realize that neither of these rationalizations were true.

During my time as a youth pastor, I received correction and revelation from the most unlikely source. A co-worker who had recently been made my supervisor checked me on some things that were not going right in my department. I had made some unpopular decisions and failed in some other areas. In the process, I ended up hurting some people to the point that my character and integrity were being questioned. Upset and under a spirit of offense, I went on the defensive and began to argue my side. After a few minutes of intense debate, my supervisor ended the discussion with these words, *"People don't judge you by your intentions. They judge you by your actions."*

Though I didn't realize it at that moment, I had just received wisdom that would eventually transform my life forever. Despite my best intentions, I was finally awakened to the fact that my actions had caused the majority of the problems in my life. I could no longer pass the blame. It was time for me to take ownership of the role I had played in my circumstances. Intended or not, it really did not matter. The fruit of my behavior was still the same. Regardless of intent, my actions created the bed I eventually came to lie in. The blame for where I found myself did not rest with anyone else. Despite what I had convinced myself to believe, I was the cause of my adverse circumstances, and it was time that I accepted responsibility for my behavior. All my life, I had been blaming others for problems that I created for myself. But, through this pride-shaking correction, I was forced to go back and reevaluate every negative situation I had experienced. I was forced to face the truth that a major portion of the negativity in my life had less to do with others and more to do with me. As much as I wanted to point the finger at other people for my problems, the reality was that much of what I was going through could simply be attributed to the personal choices that I had made. Apart from my intentions, my actions caused my downfall.

Apart from my intentions, my failure to pay my car note led to its repossession. My bad credit was the result of my poor financial stewardship. The truth of the matter was simple. I could not be trusted by others to pay my bills, so bad credit was the result. My choices had created the reality I ultimately experienced. I had no one to blame but myself.

Evaluating Past Choices

Just as a cake is the end result of the mixture of ingredients that go into the baking process, negativity is often the result of the mixture of poor choices a person has made. Whenever life does not turn out the way you expect it to, it becomes imperative that you revisit the choices you mixed together that have produced the outcome you see.

> Genesis 3:17, 23-24 NIV
> 17 To Adam he said, "Because you listened to your wife and ate fruit from the tree about which I commanded you, 'You must not eat from it,' "Cursed is the ground because of you; through painful toil you will eat food from it all the days of your life. 23 So the Lord God banished him from the Garden of Eden to work the ground from which he had been taken. 24 After he drove the man out, he placed on the east side of the Garden of Eden cherubim and a flaming sword flashing back and forth to guard the way to the tree of life.

As a result of Adam's sin, he was forced to endure a life of painful toil and exile from the comforts of the Garden of Eden. Despite Adam's attempt to pass the blame to Eve, it is very clear by

God's judgment that Adam had to face the consequences for the choices he made. God placed the responsibility for Adam's disobedience back where it belonged, with Adam. Adam's negative outcome was a direct result of his own behavior, not Eve's. Though Eve did offer Adam the opportunity to sin, sinning was Adam's own personal choice. Adam could not deflect the blame for what he had chosen to do. He had to own it. The blame game is a dangerous one to play because it conveniently reassigns responsibility to others that don't deserve it. It clears the conscience of conviction for things that you had the responsibility to control. It always appears easier to blame the Devil or people for where you are in life than it is to take ownership of your actions and make changes. No matter how you try to deflect blame, always remember that negative outcomes in life will ultimately be determined by your own choices to rebel against God's required standards.

By lumping every adversity under the banner of the *"Devil,"* most people distribute blame to whatever external source they can find. Avoiding personal responsibility gives the enemy far more credit than he deserves for the direction your life takes. Truth necessitates that you stop looking outward and begin looking inward. Where you are and where you are going can only be determined by the divine will of God over your life and the personal choices you decide to make. The reason why many people are overtaken by the Devil's schemes is not because he has authority over them but because they choose to relinquish their power to him by the choices they make.

> The reason why many people are overtaken by the Devil's schemes is not because he has authority over them but because they choose to relinquish their power to him by the choices they make.

Here is a news flash for you: Satan is only as powerful as you make him. The enemy is powerless to the person who walks in obedience to the will of God.

Colossians 2:13-15 NIV
13 When you were dead in your sins and in the uncircumcision of your flesh, God made you alive with Christ. He forgave us all our sins, 14 having canceled the charge of our legal indebtedness, which stood against us and condemned us; He has taken it away, nailing it to the cross. 15 And having disarmed the powers and authorities, He made a public spectacle of them, triumphing over them by the cross.

Jesus spoiled and disarmed all of Satan's power and authority at the cross. The only real power the enemy has is the power of persuasion. He will try to convince you to make choices outside of God's will, thereby empowering himself to manifest negative circumstances in your life. Satan cannot make you do anything without you agreeing to do it. If you walk outside the will of God, it is because you have been led astray by your own lust and made a choice to do so. Therefore, the consequences of your actions become your own undoing, not that of the Devil or anyone else.

Deuteronomy 30:19 NIV
19 This day I call the heavens and the earth as witnesses against you that I have set before you life

and death, blessings and curses. Now choose life, so that you and your children may live.

This is life in a nutshell. Making Spirit led choices leads to life. Making flesh led choices leads to death. So, be led by The Spirit and choose life. If you find yourself in a prolonged season of frustration and failure, chances are that you have made fleshly choices somewhere along the way. Your ability to identify these choices and make the proper corrections, in both your thinking and behavior, will make all the difference in your ability to prosper in the future. Once you recognize, acknowledge, and begin to take responsibility for where you are, then you will take a giant leap forward in changing where you are going.

While this may not be what you wanted to hear, it is critical to your success moving forward. If you are ever going to come out of negative circumstances, you have to develop thick skin and learn to accept hard-to-hear criticisms that make you aware of detrimental behaviors.

> 2 Timothy 4:2-3 NIV
> 2 Preach the word; be prepared in season and out of season; correct, rebuke and encourage—with great patience and careful instruction. 3 For the time will come when people will not put up with sound doctrine. Instead, to suit their own desires, they will gather around them a great number of teachers to say what their itching ears want to hear.

One of the problems that exists in the Body of Christ is that in an effort to please people, the modern church will often neglect taking hard spiritual stances. Unfortunately, the end result is limited growth and continued dysfunction. People who really want to grow don't shun correction; they embrace it. They welcome it with joy because of the freedom and increase it produces when they are obedient to it. With that said, your ability to truly evaluate past choices ultimately boils down to one question: *"Do you really want to get better?"*

In John 5, Jesus asked a similar question to a man at the pool of Bethesda who had lain cripple thirty-eight years. Having been an invalid the majority of his life, Jesus asked him a question that every person seeking to overcome adversity needs to answer, *"Do you want to be made well?"* Any *"yes"* answer to this question requires truthful reflection concerning how you arrived where you are, as well as why you are still there. You must first determine the factors that contributed to your present state of adversity. Then you must make the necessary changes to avoid similar conditions in the future.

> John 8:32 NIV
> 32 Then you will know the truth, and the truth will set you free.

Truth is God's divine pathway to freedom. Until you are honest with yourself about where you are, you will remain in spiritual bondage. Even if you manage to exit one problem by God's grace, similar situations will soon follow due to your unwillingness to change the behavior that caused you to become bound in the first place. You can no longer afford to pass the responsibility for your situation onto someone else.

> Truth is God's divine pathway to freedom. Until you are honest with yourself about where you are, you will remain in spiritual bondage.

What role have you played in your current circumstances? What choices did you make to bring about the difficulties you now face? What decisions have you made outside of the will of God that created the environment you live in today? Failure to determine what choices led to where you currently are will only make you vulnerable to repeat the behavior and continue to experience the same bondage and failure in the future.

Taking Inventory of Intimate Spaces

Reviewing choices means that you also have to inventory the intimate spaces of your life. What are intimate spaces? Intimate spaces encompass everything and everyone that touches and influences you. It also includes everything that you touch and influence. Everything close to you needs to be evaluated. From your family members and friends, your place of employment, your hangouts and hobbies, the music you choose to listen to, all forms of media that you consume, even the church that you attend, needs to be assessed. Believe it or not, all these components have the ability to be catalysts of negativity for you.

Now, at this point, you are probably saying to yourself, *"In the last section of this chapter he challenged me to take responsibility for my choices, yet is he now saying that an outside force could play a part?"* The answer is YES. Although no one can coerce you to make any choices that you don't desire, it is possible for outside forces to influence the choices you are making.

> Hebrews 12:1 KJV
> 1 Wherefore seeing we also are compassed about with so great a cloud of witnesses, let us lay aside every weight, and the sin which doth so easily beset us, and let us run with patience the race that is set before us...

Hebrews 12 calls these influences *"weights."* Whenever you allow people or things in your life that are not in line with God's character, you can be assured that if you don't deal with them promptly and properly, the weight of their influence will eventually weaken your spirit and become a source of adversity for you. External forces can create a heaviness that, in time, wears down your spirit man, causing poor choices to become attractive and negative circumstances to become certain. Much like the ground that receives a farmer's seed, human nature will always produce, positively or negatively, the seeds that are consistently sown into it. Through your five senses, you are always receiving seed that holds the potential to either bless or hinder you. Good seed planted produces good circumstances harvested. Bad seed planted produces bad circumstances harvested. It is just that simple. Whatever you allow to be sown into your life through your intimate spaces, you can expect the same to be harvested.

Coming out of high school I could count on one hand the number of times I used profanity as a teenager. The reason wasn't because I was so morally good but because I had a father who was six foot four, 245 pounds, who would - figurative speaking - kill me if he heard me using any language that even remotely sounded foul. Because of this, I was a pretty respectful young man growing up, at least. But in leaving home for college, I found myself in an environment in which profanity was widely used. Anybody who I thought highly of routinely expressed themselves with obscenities. Cursing quickly became a constant influential weight on my life. Away from the strict standards of my father, profanity became my norm. Although I shied away from the behavior at first, the weight of the constant influence soon provided a welcoming environment for the compromise of my character. The transgression that I agreed to try out turned into the iniquity that I eventually became. A young man who once wouldn't say *"dang"* out loud in fear of being back-handed had now mastered behavior that was totally counter to the way I had been raised. A corrupt and foul mouth was the end result of unchecked intimate spaces. No one person or environment held a gun to my head and made me curse. However, the unchecked environment that I immersed myself in made it very difficult not to conform.

> 1 Corinthians 15:33 NIV
> 33 Do not be misled; bad company corrupts good character.

You may not realize that sin and the effects of sin are contagious. Sinful behavior has a way of infecting you without you even being aware that you have been infected. The word *"corrupts"* in 1 Corinthians 15:33 means to spoil. This is a powerful thought because it brings to light two truths concerning a person's character when it is subjected to compromising environments.

The first truth is that **spoiling character is hardest to detect when the character being spoiled is yours**. When things spoil over time, in your presence, they tend to let out terrible odors that you are not able to smell because you have lost your sensitivity to detect them. The more gradual the change, the less noticeable the odor. Unfortunately, I learned this truth the hard way in a humiliating moment as a teenager. One day after school, before a basketball game, I took a ride with some friends to a nearby fast food spot to get something to eat. Along the way, everyone in the car began making jokes about something stinking. Oddly enough, the only one who could not smell it was me.

> Spoiling character is hardest to detect when the character being spoiled is yours.

Windows were rolled down and heads were stuck out of them. Everyone was gasping for fresh air yet, to my amazement, no matter how hard I tried, I could not smell what they were talking about. After arriving back at the school, everyone jumped out of the car, all thanking God for being free from the torture of the smell. Still oblivious to what the smell was, I went to the locker room to get ready for my game. A little later my friend, Dexter, the point guard on my team who had also been in the car, came into the locker room and broke the news to me that I was the butt of the joke. I was the horrible odor that everyone was trying to get away from. Apparently, I had neglected to put on deodorant that morning. The smell that was coming from me was appalling to everyone around me, even though it was not noticeable to me.

The revelation of this story is that often the odor that grows on you is not easily detected by you. Human senses will generally lose their sensitivity to the environment that they have grown accustomed to. Even though an odor existed on my body, I was still unaware of it because during the growth process I had become desensitized to the smell. My horrible odor was not noticeable to me because it had become a normal part of my environment. Similarly, many have allowed negative behavior to become such a normal part of their environment that they don't see it as offensive. The more you immerse yourself in environments where compromise exists, the more acceptable compromise will become to you. Spoiled character can only be corrected when you become aware of it and take intentional steps towards change.

The second truth is that **spoiling is generally a process, not an event**. Spoiling is not always a quick occurrence. Most of the time, spoiling character happens over an extended period of time. When compromise first begins, you may not notice a change after only a day or even a week. However, you will probably see a significant difference after a few months or a year. You must be careful. Most of us don't fall for the enemy's schemes that rapidly move us far outside of who we are. Most of us fall for what are "small compromises" that slowly take us away from God's standard over time. Sin doesn't always try to entice you using major acts of disobedience right away.

> Spoiling is generally a process, not an event.

The enemy's signature tactic is to employ the craftiness of time-released, small compromises and temptations. He purposes to "spoil" you through small deviations of character, spaced out over time, so you don't recognize anything is changing. He wants you to become comfortable in your spoiling and unable to discern when your standards are being lowered.

For example: Satan won't typically pressure a non-drinker to go straight to hard liquor and drugs, but he will introduce them to an environment of friends who regularly go out for a casual drink every Friday after work. In a fun and seemingly harmless atmosphere, personal standards are easily relaxed, and values are increasingly compromised. To fit in, a first drink is taken, followed by another, and then another. Another outing leads to another drink. With every round of drinks and every event attended, comfort is established and lines are continually crossed. One decision to attend a get-together with friends eventually leads to total immersion into a culture of compromise. What started out as an experience, over time, becomes a welcome desire. One minute everything seems to be going well, and the next all hell is breaking loose because compromise has taken place in small undetectable doses.

Over the years, I've concluded that compromise does not travel alone, it travels in gangs. It is always accompanied by greater levels of temptation, seeking to introduce you to greater levels of dysfunction and pain. The goal of compromise is to take you further than you want to go and get you to pay more than you desire to pay. Once a line of standards has been crossed, be assured that other temptations will soon follow. In very unassuming ways, compromise will introduce and give rise to other temptations. With patience and persistence, the enemy seduces your flesh to take bigger and more frequent bites of the forbidden fruit of compromise, with the purpose of leading you to greater levels of dysfunction and pain.

Don't allow yourself to be lulled into being spoiled through compromise. No matter how small the transgression may seem, the enemy's desire for you is total destruction. The ultimate goal of today's small compromise is to lead you to a place of false security to kill you later. Any environment that seeks to pull you away from the will of God needs to be eliminated immediately.

> Any environment that seeks to pull you away from the will of God needs to be eliminated immediately.

This is why it is imperative, for your spiritual well-being, that you examine every area of your life. If Satan is going to bring any adversity into your life, he has to do it through some instrument of flesh. Satan is a spirit and, as previously stated, in order to operate in this physical world he has to have agreement with flesh. To touch you, he has to have a legal mode of entry into the earth, by way of a person, place, or thing.

If you can see it, hear it, talk to it, receive from it, learn from it, sow into it, or dwell in or around it, you need to examine it. If what you see in it, hear from it, sow into it, or experience from it, fails to line up with God's Word, it could be a factor in your negative circumstances. Unexamined intimate spaces are potentially cancerous to your ability to come out of adversity. Identifying and separating yourself from negative intimate spaces will prove to be invaluable in your quest to being delivered from struggles moving forward. Here are some intimate spaces to examine:

- Relationships (Family & Friends)
- Job / Business Partnerships

- Social Media / Internet Use

- Book / Subscriptions

- Music / Movies / Entertainment

- Hangouts / Hobbies

- Church MembershipSocial Organizations

Forgiving Yourself

In identifying your past mistakes, be sure to guard your heart from another trick of the enemy, guilt. In evaluating past decisions, it is very easy to get caught up in the self-destructive mindset of self-condemnation. As you reflect and review the choices you have made, Satan will always attempt to sow seeds of guilt and condemnation in your mind in an effort to make you feel unworthy of God's abiding love and favor. Do not give in to this trick. No matter what you have done, God still loves you and He is ready to restore and prosper you as you choose to walk in obedience to His will for your life. John 3:16 declares God's love for you to be so extravagant that He sent Jesus to die on the cross for you despite your sins and shortcomings. The love He has for you is so great that He sacrificed His only begotten Son out of the mere hope of you accepting His love and choosing to walk in a repentant relationship with Him.

> Jeremiah 29:11 NIV
> 11 For I know the plans I have for you," declares the Lord, "plans to prosper you and not to harm you, plans to give you hope and a future.

I have always been intrigued by the wording of Jeremiah 29:11. Notice that it never says that God *"knew"* the plans that He had for you prior to your mess ups. He has not changed His mind concerning you. God says that He *"knows"* the plans He has for you. The word *"know"* in this passage is present tense, meaning God's thoughts towards you remain solidified by love, even after your failures. Despite all your mistakes and shortcomings, God's thoughts towards you remain good. They are not thoughts meant to harm you, but to bring you to a blessed future and a prosperous ending.

> Genesis 4:6-7 NIV
> Then the Lord said to Cain, "Why are you angry? Why is your face downcast? 7 If you do what is right, will you not be accepted? But if you do not do what is right, sin is crouching at your door; it desires to have you, but you must rule over it."

When Cain brought an offering to God that was unpleasing, God asked Cain three powerful questions that many of us misunderstand. Many interpret this passage to be an angry God reprimanding Cain for his failure in meeting divine standards. In contrast to this narrative, I see a compassionate and loving God showing mercy to Cain as He offers him another opportunity to get things right. I would even go so far as to say that God was not angry with Cain. He simply would not accept less than Cain's best. God's desire was to accept and show Cain favor, just as it is for us today. This is why God ends with the question, *"If you do what is right will you not be accepted?"* Cain failed to recognize that mercy had been extended to him and, by doing so, Cain missed the opportunity to experience God's true heart of redemption and restoration.

John 3:17 NIV
17 For God did not send his Son into the world to condemn the world, but to save the world through him.

The love of God is not a condemning love. It is a compassionate and restoring love. Many of us have grown up under leadership that has attempted to scare us into Heaven by overemphasizing God's wrath and underemphasizing His love. God's love for you will always outweigh His disappointment in your shortcomings. In light of the complete sacrifice made by Jesus on the cross, there is no reason for you to waddle in condemnation for past choices. Through your faith in Jesus, every debt for sin has been paid. Every justification of righteousness has been restored. Every record of guilt has been erased. All that remains is your blood-purchased promise of a blessed life through the faith choices you make moving forward. Nothing you have ever done or ever will do surpasses the love Jesus displayed on the cross for you. Despite the mistakes of your past, God loves you unconditionally. Because of that unconditional love, He is ready to accept and show you divine favor. Don't compound the mistakes of your past with a failure to recognize and receive God's correction and invitation to do what is right. Over forty times in Scripture we find the words, *"His mercy endures forever."* Psalm 23 ends by exclaiming, *"Surely goodness and mercy shall follow me all the days of my life."* Mercy is defined here as *"the withholding of punishment that one rightfully deserves."* Goodness is defined as *"pleasant, agreeable, and prosperous."* In these definitions we can extract the nature of God's love. Goodness and mercy have been ordered to follow you through every mistake, every failure, and every bad choice for one reason: Whenever you come to yourself and choose to turn back to a loving Father, He greets you with total forgiveness and overflowing love.

> Lamentations 3:21-23 NIV
> 21 Yet this I call to mind and therefore I have hope:
> 22 Because of the Lord's great love we are not consumed, for his compassions never fail. 23 They are new every morning; great is your faithfulness.

Don't allow yourself to get stuck in the mistakes of your past. God has already forgiven you, so choose to forgive yourself. It is time for you to move forward. As a believer, purpose to endure in your faith and in the limitless graces of a loving Father. Start now, making a daily decision, to accept God's unending gift of renewed mercy. Determine to cast off the shame and self-condemnation that come from a failure to forgive yourself. Forget what is behind you and press forward in God's standard, by faith.

Changing Destructive Behavior

Just as past decisions have shaped your present, your next decisions will be the building blocks for the future you will soon have. The choices you make from this point on will either establish you in, or distance you from, the favor of God.

You don't have any control over what you have already done, but you do have control over what you do moving forward. Individual errors in judgment are not always the cause of a person's downfall. What often destroys a person is their refusal to repent and change. Although the first mind of God is to forgive and restore you, there is also a corrective hand that is encompassed in His love when His children continue in disobedience and refuse to change.

> Although the first mind of God is to forgive and restore you, there is also a corrective hand that is encompassed in His love when His children continue in disobedience and refuse to change.

Hebrews 12:4-8 NIV
4 In your struggle against sin, you have not yet resisted to the point of shedding your blood. 5 And have you completely forgotten this word of encouragement that addresses you as a father addresses his son? It says, "My son, do not make light of the Lord's discipline, and do not lose heart when he rebukes you, 6 because the Lord disciplines the one he loves, and he chastens everyone he accepts as his son." 7 Endure hardship as discipline; God is treating you as his children. For what children are not disciplined by their father? 8 If you are not disciplined—and everyone undergoes discipline—then you are not legitimate, not true sons and daughters at all.

Correction is a divine sign of sonship. Even though correction does not always feel good, please understand that it is always meant for your good. True children of God welcome His discipline and strive to make changes that honor His instructions. Whenever we actively accept correction and make changes that coincide with God's discipline, divine sonship is legitimized, and favor is released.

In looking back, Cain's poor sacrifice in Genesis 4 was not his downfall. His downfall was his continued rebellion and refusal to change wrong behavior. Cain compounded one bad decision, offering God a poor sacrifice, with another poor decision, refusing to change. Disregarding God's warning, Cain rejected God's invitation to change, and moved forward with his devious plan to kill his brother. These actions and these actions alone precipitated Cain's undoing.

> Isaiah 59:1-2 KJV
> 1 Behold, the LORD's hand is not shortened, that it cannot save; neither is his ear heavy, that it cannot hear: But your iniquities have separated between you and your God, and your sins have hid his face from you that he will not hear.

Much of the hardship we experience in life is due to our failure to change when God says to. In many ways this is the definition of iniquity: choosing to remain rebellious and unrepentant concerning the standard that God has set. To transgress or to fall short of God's standard is one thing, but to consciously live in a state of rebellion and shortfall without a heart to change is totally different. Like a good parent, God will often give us warnings and opportunities to change before He applies judgment. However, when we ignore those warnings, thinking that we are exempt from the consequences of wrong behavior, we can be assured that downfall is soon to come.

How many times have you ignored God's warnings only to regret it later? Ignored grace warnings always lead to adverse consequences down the line. A choice to change wrong behavior is a choice that avoids negative outcomes in the future. A choice to continue in wrong behavior is a choice to continue in adverse circumstances in the future.

> Romans 14:4 NIV
> 4 Who are you to judge someone else's servant? To his own master he stands or falls. And he will stand, for the LORD is able to make him stand.

Change is not always easy. If it were, there would be no reason for this book. Yet, despite the difficulty of change, know that the Lord is able to empower you to stand in His standard, if you so choose. The awesome thing about God is that He specializes in perfecting imperfect people. Noah was a drunk that God used to sustain and repopulate the entire world. Moses was a temperamental, stuttering murderer that God handpicked to deliver the children of Israel out of bondage. Rahab was a prostitute whose entire destiny was altered by one decision to change her ways and serve God. Even with all your flaws and imperfections, God is more than capable of *"making you stand"* so that you are able to fulfill the assignment for which you have been created.

Psalm 138:8 KJV
8 The LORD will perfect that which concerneth me: thy mercy, O LORD, endureth forever: forsake not the works of thine own hands.

Perfect in Psalm138:8 means to *bring to a divine end*. Webster defines *perfecting* as *"the act of bringing to a state without fault or defect, flawless; as a perfect diamond, satisfying all requirements; lacking in no essential detail."* Understand that no matter how far you have gone outside of the will of God, He is still able and willing to bring you into a perfected destiny.

To the untrained eye, a raw unfinished diamond looks like an ordinary rock, but no matter what it looks like on the outside, great value exists beneath the surface. God sees you for what He has made you to be, not for what you have been. Apart from what you are or what you have been, God still promises that He *will perfect* things concerning you. The word *will* denotes promise and covenant. When you decide to change and submit to God's instructions, you enter into a divine covenant that makes failure impossible. Through obedience, your destiny becomes set and sure. When covenant is applied, your past does not matter anymore. Even in your weakness, God's strength is perfected. In your effort to change, your weaknesses become God's proving ground of faithfulness.

There is greatness inside you that God can and will bring forth. Give Him the opportunity to show Himself strong in your life through your determination to submit to His correction and your efforts to change incorrect behavior. Today's negativity can be altered by today's decisions. Allow the choices you make each day to springboard you into a blessed tomorrow. Accept God's correction and choose to change.

CHAPTER 3

Righteous Tribulation

Luke 4:1-2, 14 NIV
1 Jesus, full of the Holy Spirit, left the Jordan and was led by the Spirit into the wilderness, 2 where for forty days he was tempted by the devil. He ate nothing during those days, and at the end of them he was hungry...

14 Jesus returned to Galilee in the power of the Spirit, and news about him spread through the whole countryside.

WHAT DO YOU DO when you have evaluated your choices, most of them seem to line up with God's will, but you still seem to be going through adverse circumstances? This is the dilemma many pioneers of faith experienced throughout scripture. Joseph, through no fault of his own, found himself sold into slavery and falsely imprisoned for over a decade of his life. Job, whom God declared, "there was no one like him in all the earth," faced circumstances so severe that his wife advised him to curse

God and die. Noah was the only man found on the earth, in his generation, who met the righteous requirements of God, yet he was forced to face over a year in confinement with smelly animals, not knowing when relief would come. Jesus, completely void of sin, found himself in circumstances so agonizing that scripture declares that He had, *"sweat drops as blood"* as He prayed in the Garden of Gethsemane.

Sometimes adverse circumstances will come despite every effort on your part to follow God's standards. You can do all the right things, yet find yourself experiencing what appears to be all the wrong outcomes. You can attend church. You can do all you can to be faithful to God's instructions yet continue to experience problem after problem. What do you do?

If you have found yourself having these sorts of moments, let me encourage you to keep standing in your faith and walking in the things of God. Breakthrough is closer than you may think. Whenever God allows you to go through a difficult season it is either to correct you or to promote you. Either way, the ultimate goal is to draw you closer to Him and to get you to the outcome He has always intended for you.

Promotion By Way of Adversity

Luke 4 reveals a very interesting, yet in many ways difficult, concept to understand: God-Ordered Adversity. All adversity is not *solely* the work of Satan. Some things you face have been orchestrated by God for the purpose of taking you to greater levels of increase. When Jesus is taken into the wilderness, notice that the Bible says that it was the Holy Spirit who led Him there, not the Devil. Many believers give the enemy far too much credit concerning the events which take place in their lives. Even when you find yourself going through adversity, it is important to keep your focus on God and rest in the fact that He is eternally in control.

When looking at the trials of Job, you hear Satan's personal confession concerning his limited power in respect to God. In theory, Satan is not even a true opponent of God. To be a true opponent of God you must first possess, at the very least, the remote possibility of defeating Him. To be an opponent of God, your existence cannot be dependent on Him.

> Some things you face have been orchestrated by God for the purpose of taking you to greater levels of increase.

Job 1:8-12 NIV
8 Then the Lord said to Satan, "Have you considered my servant, Job? There is no one on earth like him; he is blameless and upright, a man who fears God and shuns evil." 9 "Does Job fear God for nothing?" Satan replied. 10 "Have you not put a hedge around him and his household and everything he has? You have blessed the work of his hands, so that his flocks and herds are spread throughout the land. 11 But now stretch out your hand and strike everything he has, and he will surely curse you to your face." 12 The Lord said to Satan, "Very well then, everything he has is in your power, but on the man himself do not lay a finger."

The power of God, without question, is vastly superior to that of Satan. In fact, to use the word *superior* fails to scratch the surface of how much greater the power of God is than that of any spiritual force that dares oppose Him. The mere suggestion of touching Job, apart from getting permission from God, was laughable even to Satan himself. As this passage shows, God didn't even lift a finger to keep Satan away from Job. Job's alignment with God's standard and God's divine presence was enough to create a hedge of protection for him that could not be breached.

No power exists unless God allows it to exist. Every authority and power is subject to The Lord. No one is equal or worthy of being mentioned in the same breath as His greatness. God is so awesome and infinitely superior to everyone, that mere words fail to do Him justice.

To further illustrate this point, take particular notice of the wording Job 1:11 uses as the scene unfolds. *"But put forth THINE HAND and strike everything he has, and he will surely curse you to your face."* This wording is interesting because it suggests that even when Satan has been released by the Lord to touch the life of a believer, the hand of God is still at work in the equation. A clear parallel is made here between the things Satan wanted to do against Job and the hand of God still being in operation in Job's life. One can conclude that no matter what circumstances exist, good or bad, God's hand and purpose are still at work on your behalf. Any move of the enemy is a move that God is aware of and one that He has allowed to benefit you. At all times, what Satan means for evil, God already has a plan established for good. God has no equal. He is not challenged or stopped by anything Satan tries to do. Satan is completely subject to the sovereignty of God.

> Any move of the enemy is a move that God is aware of and one that He has allowed to benefit you.

Therefore, when you strive to operate in God's will, know that the enemy only can come against you to the degree that God releases him. Whenever you see Satan and the adverse circumstances he attempts to bring your way, confidently assume that God is up to something big. Challenges in life cannot be summed up as being solely the attacks of the enemy. When we do so, we are undervaluing God's divine sovereignty. Despite the attacks, know that the sovereign plan of the Lord is always being executed.

Be assured, Satan does not operate on *"stealth mode."* He does not possess the ability to move independently or void of the permissive will of God. Whenever the enemy moves in the earth, every move is limited by God's supreme authority. Nothing happens outside of God's knowing. Everything you face is a part of God's well thought out plan to bring Him glory. Start seeing adversity for what it really is. Adversity is a setup by the Holy Spirit to promote you to another level of glory and increase. Job went into his adversity at one level of prosperity, yet he came out with a double portion. What areas of your life has God ordered increase on the other side of your adversity? How might God have purposed to grow you in wisdom, understanding, influence, or anointing? What things could God have decided to double up on your behalf based on how you manage adverse moments?

Justification For Promotion

Now you may ask, *"If God wants to promote me, why doesn't He just do so? Why does promotion have to come through adversity?"* Good question! The answer can be found in *"The Requirement of Faith."* Promotion is not something that is simply given without reason. Promotion is usually earned. In the business world, truly successful businesses don't promote you for the sake of it. Good businesses promote employees who have shown proficiency and faithfulness at lower levels. When *"just cause"* for promotion is shown, promotion is granted. The same is true for Kingdom business.

> Matthew 25:21 NIV
> 21 His master replied, 'Well done, good and faithful servant! You have been faithful with a few things; I will put you in charge of many things. Come and share your master's happiness!'

Though many desire promotion, most don't receive it because they lack the faithfulness required to obtain it. If you can't be faithful in adversity, why should God promote you to the next level? The key to elevation tomorrow is mastery of where you are today. Whenever you develop the ability to maintain faithfulness where you are, God releases you to the next level.

> Romans 1:17 KJV
> 17 For therein is the righteousness of God revealed from faith to faith: as it is written, the just shall live by faith.

Justification is a product of man's faith. You cannot purchase justification. You cannot obtain it by way of good deeds. Justification is only obtained when you choose to operate in the principles of faith. Faith justifies you for promotion in the eyes of God. So, if faith is a justification for promotion, then adverse conditions, which require a faith response, become necessary. Adversity is the environment that provides you the opportunity to please God through your faith response. For this reason, properly stewarding adversity becomes critical. Recognize adversity for what it is: a God-ordained plan to elevate and bless you. Your promotion to greater levels of divine purpose is directly related to your determination to endure in faith through all that you are going through.

> Luke 4:14 NIV
> 14 Jesus returned to Galilee in the power of the Spirit, and news about him spread through the whole countryside.

At the beginning of Luke 4, Jesus enters the wilderness *"full of the Spirit."* However, by the end of the chapter, Jesus returns from the wilderness *"in the power of the Spirit."* Even Jesus endured a level of adversity to obtain the justification to move into the next level of empowerment. The wilderness was the environment that God ordered for Jesus to transition from potential to power. Likewise, at the end of Jesus's earthly ministry, His endurance of the cross allowed Him to be exalted to God's right hand. Whatever adverse circumstance you encounter, know that faithful endurance is the doorway to your next level of divine blessings.

When first sharing the concept of God-Ordained Adversity with respected friends in the faith, I received strong rebuke from some of them. One, in particular, offered an aggressive challenge to any idea of a loving God allowing His children to experience any level of discomfort. He concluded that it was out of God's nature and character to be a part of any level of suffering concerning His children, for any reason. He said that if the nature of God was to heal, deliver, and prosper, why would He be a part of ordaining negative circumstances in their lives? He then challenged my position as a father by asking the question, *"Would you allow pain and discomfort in the lives of your children if you had the power to prevent it?"*

I have to tell you, when posed with this question, my writing quickly came to a screeching halt. As I looked at my children running around the house, it became truly difficult for me to remain stable in my belief that a loving Father would allow pain or discomfort to come upon His children. I was truly stumped. Part of me was in total agreement that I would not allow my children to experience hurt of any kind, yet a voice inside me (The Holy Spirit) continued to scream, *"Press Deeper! Press Deeper! You are on the right track."* So I did, and here is what God showed me.

God of Priority

> 3 John 2 KJV
> 2 Beloved, I wish above all things that thou mayest prosper and be in health, even as thy soul prospereth.

"Above all things..." God desires for you to have every good thing and to always abound in good health. Without a doubt, it is not the will of God for you to be in lack. Without question, it is not His desire for you to be in pain. John makes it clear that God's perfect will is that you always operate from a position of peace and blessings. However, it is critical for the maturity of believers that we also see what is most important to God in this scripture. Though God unquestionably wants you to prosper and be in good physical health, the greater passion of His heart is for you to prosper in your soul. The words *"even as"* establishes salvation as God's leading priority over personal comfort. Though your comfort and health are extremely important to God, your soul always takes precedence. When God's perfect will is not accepted by those He loves, His permissive will is applied. This is to establish His ultimate priority of salvation in the lives of His children. Temporary discomfort now is far better than eternal damnation later. God places greater priority on the destination of your soul than He does on the comfort of your flesh. When addressing immoral sexual behavior in the church of Corinth, Paul advises church leaders to hand an individual over to Satan so that his body can be destroyed, but his soul saved. Sometimes temporary discomfort of the flesh is necessary to avoid eternal torment of a person's soul.

> Temporary discomfort now is far better than damnation later. God places greater priority on the destination of your soul than He does on the comfort of your flesh.

You may be asking yourself, *"Well, what if I am already saved? What need would God have to allow negative circumstances in my life?"* The answer to those questions can be found in the same revelation God gave me when debating my qualifications to write this book, *"It is not about you."* Sometimes the adversity that you face has less to do with you and is more about the salvation of those around you.

I call this the "Living Bible Factor." Sometimes God allows you to go through adverse circumstances to set an example for others. God will permit discomfort in your life to create opportunities for others to get a revelation concerning who He is by how you handle the situation. In Daniel 3, we see this point on full display. Here, three Hebrew men are faced with a difficult choice: bow to an idol and live or hold to their faith in God and die. Without hesitation, all three men chose the latter.

> Daniel 3:19-20, 24-25 NKJV
> 19 Then Nebuchadnezzar was full of fury, and the expression on his face changed toward Shadrach, Meshach, and Abednego. He spoke and commanded that they heat the furnace seven times more than it was usually heated. 20 And he commanded certain mighty men of valor who were in his army to bind Shadrach, Meshach, and Abednego, and cast them into the burning fiery furnace.
>
> 24 Then King Nebuchadnezzar was astonished; and he rose in haste and spoke, saying to his counselors, "Did we not cast three men bound into the midst of the fire?" They answered and said to the king, "True, O king."25 "Look!" he answered, "I see four men loose, walking in the midst of the fire; and they are not hurt, and the form of the fourth is like the Son of God."

This passage clearly expresses how and why God uses difficult circumstances evangelistically. The resolve of Shadrach, Meshach, and Abedego to hold to their faith in the face of their impending death ultimately enabled an idol-worshipping king to receive a revelation about God that he hadn't before. In this moment, God shifted the heart of King Nebuchadnezzar so much so that his testimony became *"there is no other God who is able to rescue in this way (Daniel 3:29)."* Therefore, through three men's adversity, an earthly king was moved to an eye-opening awareness of God's authenticity and power, ultimately affecting an entire region of people.

God's love has been extended to the world, not just to you as an individual. His heart is that none would perish. Thus, He will often use your life, as an individual, to reveal His corporate love for the masses. Like Jesus at Calvary, the cross of the believer is not always about him or her. The soldier at the foot of the cross, after seeing how Jesus suffered, declared in amazement, *"Surely this was the Son of God."* Rather than being about you, much of what you go through is about a faith in God, and a revelation of God, that others get when they witness how you endure.

> Romans 8:18-21 NIV
> 18 I consider that our present sufferings are not worth comparing with the glory that will be revealed in us. 19 For the creation waits in eager expectation for the children of God to be revealed. 20 For the creation was subjected to frustration, not by its own choice, but by the will of the one who subjected it, in hope 21 that the creation itself will be liberated from its bondage to decay and brought into the freedom and glory of the children of God.

As a believer, you will be subjected daily to frustrating circumstances. This is life. However, be assured that your vexation is not without purpose. It has been ordained by God as a tool of liberation. How you navigate adversity is meant to be a visible testimony of what God can do in others' lives. God often uses the difficult experiences of His children as roadmaps for unbelievers to reference as they seek to find their way to God. The only question is, can you stand to go through adversity so that someone else can get a revelation about God that sets them free from bondage and sin? Remember the old saying, "You may be the only Bible someone will ever read."

God Of Sovereignty and Omnipotence

The mistake most people make when they attempt to understand God using adversity for His glorify, is that they try to determine what God would or would not do based on human logic and man's natural limitations. It is impossible to figure out what God would do using these methods because it attempts to lower God's supernatural attributes. God's ways are not natural. His ways are not our ways, and His thoughts are not our thoughts. So, to make a determination about God from this limited perspective will never produce an accurate assessment of what He would do. To know what God would do, you first have to understand His divine attributes as well as how those attributes differ from man's.

Man is a finite being. This means that he is limited in both capacity and function. Man is powerless on his own. The notion of allowing a loved one to go through discomfort is harder to grasp for natural man because of his limited ability to rescue, save, or deliver. On the other hand, God is both Elohim and Jehovah. He is both supreme creator and all-powerful loving Father. He is omnipresent and omnipotent. Simply put, there is no situation that intimidates God. In Him exists both the ultimate authority and power to control and change any situation without limitations. God has never been, nor ever will be, moved by the presumed negative conditions of man. No matter how bad a situation is to you, God always can deliver you from whatever He allows you to go through.

> John 11:1-6 NIV
> 1 Now a man named Lazarus was sick. He was from Bethany, the village of Mary and her sister Martha. 2 (This Mary, whose brother Lazarus now lay sick, was the same one who poured perfume on the Lord and wiped his feet with her hair.) 3 So the sisters sent word to Jesus, "Lord, the one you love is sick." 4 When he heard this, Jesus said, "This sickness will not end in death. No, it is for God's glory so that God's Son may be glorified through it." 5 Now Jesus loved Martha and her sister and Lazarus. 6 So when he heard that Lazarus was sick, he stayed where he was two more days, 7 and then he said to his disciples, "Let us go back to Judea."

In John 11, Jesus is sent a message that His good friend Lazarus was dying. Upon receiving this news, Jesus had both the desire and the ability to go right away to see about Lazarus, yet scripture declares that He waited two more days. The question is, why? Why did Jesus wait a whole two days before going to the aid of a friend? The answer is simple, He could. In a crisis, time usually works against natural man. But with God, it is just the opposite, time works for Him. Jesus waited an extra two days because He did not operate in the constraints of natural man. Jesus allowed Lazarus to die to destroy the earthly limitations that had been placed on His divinity by those who thought they knew Him. After Lazarus was raised from the dead, all who witnessed his resurrection began to know Jesus in a different way. Because of the adversity Jesus delayed in coming to, each bystander went to another level of faith concerning who they knew Jesus to be. Before Lazarus' death, Mary believed Jesus to be the resurrection of the future, but after Lazarus was raised, she knew Jesus as the resurrection of the present. Mary's inadequate understanding of who Jesus was greatly shifted because of the adversity she endured.

During a very stressful season of my life, I found myself homeless, carrying everything I owned around in two duffle bags. I was desperately searching for answers. One cold winter's night, not wanting to sleep outside, I called a friend from a pay phone and began sharing my struggles. As I was talking, I discovered that a man at the pay phone next to mine was listening intently to my conversation. In the process of me talking, he interrupted to tell me that he had a place where I could stay for a few nights. Not fully confident in the offer, yet desperate for somewhere to sleep other than my car, I followed him to an old, dilapidated duplex that He claimed to be a rental house that he owned. He offered to let me stay there for a few days until the cold weather passed. As he unlocked the door and allowed me inside, what I saw made me strongly reconsider my decision. Baseball-sized holes adorned every window. The carpet on the floor was covered with a thick, nasty film of bird feces and mildew. There was no furniture, except for an old filthy mattress, so soiled and dirty that when you hit it dust flew into the air. This place was totally unfit for anyone to occupy. Nevertheless, as bad as it was, it did offer a slight relief from the gusting winds outside. Using a few of the clothes I had, I covered the mattress the best I could. Then, in tears, I lay down, placing the remainder of my clothes over my head and body to keep warm. That night, I cried out to God like never before, only to hear these four words, *"I will restore you."* Not fully understanding what those words meant, I left that duplex a few days later and never returned.

Over the next few years, God took me on a day-by-day journey of learning that transitioned me out of homelessness and into ministry at a thriving urban church congregation in Downtown Houston, Texas. After serving as the youth pastor there for three months, I was given my first opportunity to preach at a 12 o'clock Sunday service. I fasted, I prayed, I studied, and I prepared. I walked up to the podium, facing the largest congregation that I had ever spoken in front of, and I heard these words, *"Consider yourself restored."* At that moment I began to cry and give thanks to God for His faithfulness. I realized that through every experience, positive or negative, I was now standing in God's ordained place of blessing. Though it was not the route that I would have chosen for myself, God used every circumstance to reveal dimensions of Himself that I had never known existed. Every test had produced a testimony. Every problem had given way to empowerment. Every obstacle revealed a divine opportunity. Because of what I went through, an intimacy with God and a trust in Him developed, the likes of which I never thought possible. Through an extremely painful season of life, a faith was birthed which is the stabilizing source of everything I am today.

Hebrews 12:1-2 NIV
1 Therefore, since we are surrounded by such a great cloud of witnesses, let us throw off everything that hinders and the sin that so easily entangles.

And let us run with perseverance the race marked out for us, 2 fixing our eyes on Jesus, the pioneer and perfecter of faith. For the joy set before him he endured the cross, scorning its shame, and sat down at the right hand of the throne of God.

Man views adversity through the perspective of pain that exists in moments, but God views adversity through the perspective of the eternal joy and hope that is produced through faithful endurance. Just as God got glory out of Christ's endurance of the cross by raising Him from the dead, God will also get glory out of your life as you trust Him to raise you from every difficult situation.

Please understand that I am not suggesting that God is the cause of adverse circumstances in the lives of His children. God did not cause me to be homeless, nor did He cause Lazarus to die. However, I am saying that in His sovereign will, God allows and uses adversity to bring about His ultimate purpose for those He loves. As a father, the natural man would not allow their child to go through adversity because of his inability to control the outcome, but God allows his children to go through adversity because of the power He possesses to deliver them from it. Unlike man, God has the unique ability to weave His divine plan into the attacks of the enemy so that those who come out of it do so with a greater revelation of who He is.

CHAPTER 4

Divine Transition

GOD NEVER INTENDS FOR adversity to be your final destination. He actually wants it to be a place of divine transition. Adversity is never meant to be your end but a means to an end. Trust that where you are isn't where you will always be. God has led you here for the purpose of transitioning you to the next level of blessing in your life. Generally, seasons of divine transition can be categorized in two ways:

1. You are operating outside of the will of God and He allows adversity for the purpose of transitioning you out of darkness back into the light of His perfect will.

2. God allows adversity for the purpose of validating you to transition into greater levels of revelation and faith in Him.

In both cases, the purpose of adversity is always transition, never destruction.

One harsh reality that is rarely talked about concerning divine transitions is though they are often celebrated when prophesied, divine transitions are frequently despised during the process. We like to hear and receive prophetic words of increase spoken over our lives, but most prophetic words never seem to fully explain the difficulty of the transition that awaits. The alluring thought of the prophetic end is one that makes every person rejoice with great anticipation, but the time between the prophecy and its manifestation is oftentimes very challenging and difficult.

> Genesis 37:5-8 NIV
> 5 Joseph had a dream, and when he told it to his brothers, they hated him all the more. 6 He said to them, "Listen to this dream I had: 7 We were binding sheaves of grain out in the field when suddenly my sheaf rose and stood upright, while your sheaves gathered around mine and bowed down to it." 8 His brothers said to him, "Do you intend to reign over us? Will you actually rule us?" And they hated him all the more because of his dream and what he had said.

> Genesis 42:6-7 NIV
> 6 Now Joseph was the governor of the land, the person who sold grain to all its people. So, when Joseph's brothers arrived, they bowed down to him with their faces to the ground. 7 As soon as Joseph saw his brothers, he recognized them...

Genesis 37 shows Joesph enjoying the comforts of his father's home while having a dream concerning his future status of authority. Nowhere in his dream did he foresee the difficulty ordained for him to acquire this power. He endured extreme jealousy and rejection at the hands of his brothers. He was left for dead in a wilderness pit and sold into multiple levels of slavery. Joseph was even unjustly imprisoned and had to watch over a decade of his life pass away before he ever got the opportunity to walk in the destiny he saw in his dream. Though God did reveal the glory-filled ending to Joseph beforehand, what was not shown to him was the impending struggle of the process. 1 Corinthians 13:9 teaches us that God frequently reveals prophesies *"in part."* The *"why?"* behind this scripture is that most people can't handle the *"full"* picture if God decided to share it with them. God will often withhold details of the journey due to our immaturity. He will show us glimpses of the ending glory because it inspires us to run, yet He will just as often withhold details of the process, so that we don't become discouraged from saying yes to the call.

Divine transitions are very rarely short, easy rides. They are usually long, lonely, difficult, faith-building journeys that shake the foundation of everything in which you believe and trust. Divine transitions exhaust patience, perceived resources, and time, as well as established relationships, until all that remains is your faith in a promise that was planted in your spirit by God. The promise is often directly opposite to the natural reality that you see, and it is out of this place of conflict that you must learn to hold onto the understanding that what you are facing is only a transition, not an eternal reality. Your hope has to become solidified in more than your personal qualifications and merit. It must become grounded in an internal resolve to trust God's faithfulness to do what He said He would do.

Leading Role

Whenever I have free time, one of the things I enjoy doing most is sitting down and relaxing with a good movie. New or old, action or drama, if it has a good story line I want to see it. Knowing my love for movies, my younger sister bought me one of the most incredible birthday gifts ever, a five-volume set of the "Rocky Series." Since Rocky is my favorite movie series of all-time, I could now watch it as many times as I wanted, whenever I wanted. One evening while watching Rocky III, an epic scene in the movie sparked a profound revelation concerning adversity and transitional seasons. Approximately a third of the way through the movie, under great duress due to the sickness of his beloved trainer and father figure, Mickey, Rocky enters the ring with Clubber Lang (aka Mr. T) for what was to be his final boxing match before retiring. Unable to withstand the power of the bigger challenger, Rocky suffers a brutal knockout in the second round. Afterwards, bruised and battered, Rocky returns to his dressing room, only to find Mickey gasping for breath, eventually dying in Rocky's arms, stretched out on a cold trainer's table. At that moment, an interesting question came up in my spirit concerning the movie, *"How do you know that the movie is not over?"* I paused the movie because I knew this question was deeper than the obvious answer that I had seen it before. So, I asked, *"How?"* Immediately, a simple but profound thought dropped in my heart that changed how I look at adversity forever. The answer that followed was this, *"Because Rocky has not won yet!"*

> Ephesians 2:6-7 NIV
> 6 And God raised us up with Christ and seated us with him in the heavenly realms in Christ Jesus, 7 in order that in the coming ages he might show the incomparable riches of his grace, expressed in his kindness to us in Christ Jesus.

As you face various levels of adversity, it is crucial to keep in mind the thoughts God has towards you (Jeremiah 29:11). They are thoughts of peace and good, not thoughts of failure. God's thoughts concerning you are rooted in His desire to see you take hold of a blessed future. As the Author and Finisher of your faith, be assured that God's mind is driven by His unfailing love for you. His intentions are to fulfill His covenant promise by displaying the riches of His grace and kindness in your life. Thus, any condition that you find yourself in that does not resemble love and peace cannot be the end of the story.

> Any condition that you find yourself in that does not resemble love and peace cannot be the end of the story.

Rocky was not victorious yet, so the story could not be over. Likewise, you are the "Lead Supporting Actor" God has cast for this glorious role of triumph *(Jesus is the Lead Actor)*. Know that walking out God's scripted destiny for your life will not end until you come to the victorious outcome that He has always intended.

2 Corinthians 4:7-10, 15-18 NIV
7 But we have this treasure in jars of clay to show that this all-surpassing power is from God and not from us. 8 We are hard pressed on every side, but not crushed; perplexed, but not in despair; 9 persecuted, but not abandoned; struck down, but not destroyed. 10 We always carry around in our body the death of Jesus, so that the life of Jesus may also be revealed in our body...

15 All this is for your benefit, so that the grace that is reaching more and more people may cause thanksgiving to overflow to the glory of God. 16 Therefore we do not lose heart. Though outwardly we are wasting away, yet inwardly we are being renewed day by day. 17 For our light and momentary troubles are achieving for us an eternal glory that far outweighs them all. 18 So we fix our eyes not on what is seen, but on what is unseen, since what is seen is temporary, but what is unseen is eternal.

When you are going through adversity, make sure to never overlook the obvious. Despite every blow taken, you are still here. You might be bruised and a little beat up, but you are still breathing. Through every perplexing situation, you are still able to stand if you choose to. Having done all to stand, choose to stand firm. You have survived through things others have not. You have endured circumstances that caused someone else to give up. You have bounced back from disappointment after disappointment and have remained steadfast through attacks that have seen others lose their minds. Through it all, you are still alive. The very fact that you have not been taken out should give you some indication that your story is not over and there is more to be told.

2 Corinthians 4:7 gives us insight into why we feel so inferior in the face of adversity. This feeling of insufficiency cannot be solely attributed to the enemy. *"In my weakness, His strength is made perfect (2 Corinthians 12:9-10)."* This feeling has been purposed by God to continuously remind us of our total dependence on Him. Grasping this truth will help you remain anchored in faith, with your belief system based on the fullness of who He is, rather than

on who you are. You have been gifted the privilege of carrying the death of Jesus in your body so that His glory will be on full display when He triumphantly resurrects your life in seasons to come. Don't grow weary in well doing. You will get the breakthrough if you do not give up. Hold onto your faith. All that you are facing will soon prove beneficial for you. Believe it or not, the weight of your struggle can't be compared to the glory that God has scripted for you in the end.

Let's continue to explore Rocky. Suffering a vicious knockout at the hands of Clubber Lang in their first fight, Rocky was forced to come to a simple resolve before stepping back into the ring a second time. He determined that one fight did not define the war. Rocky's loss to Lang didn't signify the end of the story. It actually indicated the beginning of a dramatic transition to a victorious outcome, pre-scripted by the author. As the movie continued to unfold, Rocky accepted the challenge to keep fighting. Facing his fears, surrounded by a new support system, he began to train harder than he ever had before. Through the process, fear gave way to faith and depression gave way to determination. Rocky stepped into the second fight with Lang a totally different man. He was a more confident and more determined version of his former self. He had endured through a difficult scene, finding himself at the start of the predetermined victory he was always purposed to walk in. This time, motivated to press forward through an even greater barrage of Lang's attacks, the end of the second fight saw Rocky showered by the cheers of clamoring fans, victory in hand. With the once seemingly unbeatable foe slumped dejected in his corner, Lang was defeated, never to be heard from again. Rocky was once again the Heavyweight Champion of the World. End of story!

> Romans 8:28-30 NIV
> 28 And we know that in all things God works for the good of those who love him, who have been called according to his purpose. 29 For those God foreknew He also predestined to be conformed to the image of his Son, that He might be the firstborn among many brothers and sisters. 30 And those He predestined, He also called; those He called, He also justified; those He justified, He also glorified.

Every situation in your life is not going to feel good, but it will work out for your good, if you choose to accept this truth. The purpose of every circumstance in life is to bring you one step closer to the image of Christ. As He has been glorified, you have been called and justified to experience that glory in Him as well. Don't give up before God is able to unfold His scripted end for your life. Be careful not to mistake a scene in your story for the end of the story. Develop an awareness in your spirit that you are not crushed, you are not hopeless, you are not destroyed or abandoned by God. You are only in a moment of divine transition that will soon give way to a victorious ending. Adversity has taken its best shot. Shake it off! Find the courage to fight another day knowing God is not done with you.

The Grace of Goshen

> Exodus 8:20-28 NIV
> 20 Then the Lord said to Moses, "Get up early in the morning and confront Pharaoh as he goes to the river and say to him, 'This is what the Lord says: Let my people go, so that they may worship me. 21

> If you do not let my people go, I will send swarms of flies on you and your officials, on your people, and into your houses. The houses of the Egyptians will be full of flies; even the ground will be covered with them. 22 'But on that day I will deal differently with the land of Goshen, where my people live; no swarms of flies will be there, so that you will know that I, the Lord, am in this land. 23 I will make a distinction between my people and your people. This sign will occur tomorrow.'" 24 And the Lord did this...

While the area around Israel experienced great distress and destruction, God made a clear distinction between Goshen, where Israel lived, and the rest of Egypt. With all the plagues released to devastate Egypt, by God's grace, many were not allowed to affect Israel's place of dwelling. As the hand of God could clearly be seen against territories under Pharaoh's rule, that same hand could also be seen protecting Goshen from the full impact of the plagues. In the season of Israel's greatest oppression, they also experienced one of the greatest outpourings of grace anyone has ever witnessed. As Pharaoh helplessly watched the decimation of Egypt due to disease, pestilence, and supernatural occurrences, Goshen remained sustained by God's protection and provisional grace.

No matter how bad things may appear to be on the surface, grace is always at work. Although you may feel you are in a desperate situation, understand that if it were not for the grace of God things could be a whole lot worse. In moments of self-pity, it is easy to become so focused on what is wrong in your life that you fail to see and appreciate what is right.

Psalm 100 NIV

1 Shout for joy to the Lord, all the earth. 2 Worship the Lord with gladness; come before Him with joyful songs. 3 Know that the Lord is God. It is He who made us, and we are His; we are His people, the sheep of His pasture. 4 Enter His gates with thanksgiving and His courts with praise; give thanks to Him and praise His name. 5 For the Lord is good and His love endures forever; His faithfulness continues through all generations.

Psalm 100 gives us a description of a believer's journey into the presence of God. Verse 4 provides a picture of the three courts of the Temple of Moses that Israel was commanded to erect at each stop along their journey to the Promised Land. These three courts consisted of The Outer Courts, The Inner Courts, and The Holy of Holies.

In the first court, The Outer Court, two furnishings could be found that provide significant revelation concerning God's grace in the midst of adversity. The first of these furnishings was the Bronze Altar. It was a structure on which sacrifices were made, publicly, to God for the covering of sin. The Outer Court was the bloodiest area in the temple. It was an area of the temple where things came to die. It is in this court that Psalm 100 says we are to enter in with thanksgiving and praise. This

> In moments of self-pity, it is easy to become so focused on what is wrong in your life that you fail to see and appreciate what is right.

is incredibly profound in that it reveals the requirement of a thankful heart even in times of great sacrifice. In moments when things are being consumed by the fires of life, spiritual maturity still holds its character and finds a reason to praise God. Anyone can acknowledge grace in places of abundance and blessings, but can you recognize grace and maintain a thankful heart in times when things are dying around you? Can you voice your praise when discomfort is at its highest? Isaiah modeled this maturity for us when he declared, *"In the year that King Uzziah died, I saw the Lord, high and exalted, seated on a throne, and His robe filled the temple."* Mature believers don't allow circumstances to dictate how they see God. In the midst of adversity, maturity recognizes an eternal God who is still on His throne. His majesty does not decrease with the onset of adversity. God was God before things became difficult for you, and He remains God in the midst of things being difficult. Know with certainty that God will never cease being God. He was God before, He is God during, and He will be God long after difficulty is over. The only question is, will you maintain a heart of thanksgiving through it?

The second piece of furnishing found in the Outer Court was The Bronze Laver. This piece was a large water basin that was used for ceremonial washing after sacrifices were offered on the Bronze Altar. It represented a place of qualification and sanctification; a picture of the washing God does in believers as He gives them a new heart and a new nature. This receptacle was set up only a short distance from the Bronze Altar where sacrifices were made. This is significant in that it indicates the ability for your spirit to prosper in the same season and the same environment that your flesh is dying. In the shadows of great external afflictions, maturity is the ability to appreciate God for the internal work He is doing to prosper the spirit. All too often believers make the crucial mistake of defining grace by the world's standards. They make grace out to be solely the accumulation of physical wealth and possessions, but grace is much more than materialism. Grace is often expressed as an increase in spiritual wisdom and an increase in submission to God's standard. Other times it is shown through the protective hand of God existing over one's life, even when you are unaware of it. Still other times, it is seen in ways that may be overlooked because it is impossible to quantify, like spiritual maturity, divine wisdom, peace, and contentment. Consequently, grace is often dismissed as insignificant when it is actually the thing we should desire the most and be most thankful for.

As a young adult, fresh out of college, I had the wonderful fortune of attending a dynamic ministry in Augusta, Georgia named Beulah Grove Baptist Church, at that time under the pastoral leadership of Dr. Sam Davis. Dr. Davis and The Grove, as it was affectionally called, were without question foundational pillars that helped shape my spiritual journey. I remember one Sunday, Dr. Davis shared a message on "The Ability to Find Grace In Every Situation." In the sermon, I distinctly recall him giving a comical example of how to find grace, even in the most difficult circumstances. He said...

"What if your dog dies? Where is the Grace in that? Well, with the price of dog food these days, just think how much money you are going to save by not having to feed it anymore." ~ Dr. Sam Davis

As crazy as this example may have sounded, the truth it expressed was very powerful. No matter how difficult a situation may be, there is always a degree of grace in everything you go through. Life will always give you a reason to feel defeated and deflated if you are looking for one. If you choose to look for something to be depressed about, be assured that you will quickly be given a reason. Conversely, know that if you choose to look for a reason to be hopeful, if you choose to look for God, you will find Him.

> Philippians 4:8 NIV
> 8 Finally, brothers and sisters, whatever is true, whatever is noble, whatever is right, whatever is pure, whatever is lovely, whatever is admirable – if anything is excellent or praiseworthy – think about such things.

Purpose to find reasons to believe. Open your eyes to things that are worthy of giving God praise. Circumstances may not be what you want them to be, but God is still excellent and worthy of being exalted. As uncomfortable as captivity was in Goshen, the grace of God was still at work on Israel's behalf. God was still worthy. In the same way, as uncomfortable as your circumstances may be, God's grace is still at work on your behalf, and that is more than enough to focus on and believe in.

Redefining Success

As God begins to accelerate you into the ordained victory He has for you, please understand that it may not look like the end you foresaw for yourself. Most people make the mistake of attempting to define success by the world's standards. Success is often equated to the lifestyles of the rich and famous, defined by how much you have or by how comfortable you are. God's view of success is totally different.

Luke 23:44-46 NIV

44 It was now about noon, and darkness came over the whole land until three in the afternoon, 45 for the sun stopped shining. And the curtain of the temple was torn in two. 46 Jesus called out with a loud voice, "Father, into your hands I commit my spirit." When he had said this, he breathed his last.

Due to the many signs, wonders, and miracles of Jesus' public ministry, He is often referred to by believers as the essence of success. He is consistently held up as the standard for true achievement. While this assessment of Jesus is completely accurate, it is amazing that this standard of success that most attest to is frequently not the standard of success that they seek for themselves. At the moment of Jesus' transition from earth to glory, the ministry He walked in had no semblance of anything we would consider successful. As blood streamed from His body, as He hung on a cross dying, nothing about Jesus' life resembled anything typically associated with success. Natural wealth was not present, and no one considered Him to be a person to be envied. In fact, as much as it is said that everyone has a cross to bear, I would venture to bet that no one would have wanted to change places with Jesus in that moment. Though He fulfilled every requirement of the calling of God on His life, as He hung dying on a Roman cross, Jesus' success was clothed in a bruised and bloodied body, betrayal, shame and rejection by the very people that He came to save. By today's standards, He would be the disgraced minister, with all His followers walking away, not even caring to speak up on His behalf. He would be the fallen pastor whose congregation became scattered after He was arrested and convicted, despite unproven claims of wrongdoing. He would have been target #1 of every national tabloid and the punchline of every late-night talk show monologue. By all accounts, He would have been considered an absolute failure by the world's standards, but not by God. Despite the world's criteria, Jesus is still the Savior of the world, The Son of God, and the perfect example of success.

This thought brings up some interesting questions. What if the success God has purposed for you turns out to look nothing like the picture of success the world offers you? More importantly, what if the success God has ordained for you looks nothing like the picture of success you have dreamed for yourself? What if God calls you to a success without recognition or applause? What if God calls you to minister to small groups or individuals, but never to the multitudes? What if the abundance God wants to bless you with comes in packages of wisdom and revelation, but never through financial streams? Are you okay with accepting a version of success that is not as glamorous as you might have dreamed, yet it pleases God? Are you okay with a calling that prospers God's Kingdom more than it prospers you?

> Many times, the problem is not where you are in life. The problem exists in failing to accept God's view of success instead of your own.

A huge key in transitioning out of adversity is learning to redefine and to accept what true success is. Many times, the problem is not where you are in life. The problem exists in failing to accept God's view of success instead of your own. In one moment, you say to God, *"Let Your will be done in my life,"* but in the next moment, when circumstances fail to line up with your definition of success, you quickly reject where you are in search of a place of greater personal comfort.

Although wealth, applause, and acceptance are all benchmarks for the world's view of success, these things are frequently absent from a God-ordained call.

> Matthew 5:3-10 NIV
> 3 "Blessed are the poor in spirit, for theirs is the kingdom of heaven. 4 Blessed are those who mourn, for they will be comforted. 5 Blessed are the meek, for they will inherit the earth. 6 Blessed are those who hunger and thirst for righteousness, for they will be filled. 7 Blessed are the merciful, for they will be shown mercy. 8 Blessed are the pure in heart, for they will see God. 9 Blessed are the peacemakers, for they will be called children of God. 10 Blessed are those who are persecuted because of righteousness, for theirs is the kingdom of heaven.

Don't become so driven by the world's standards of success and blessings that you forget that God's standard of success looks totally different. True success means that you are fully submitted to God's will over your own. It is measured by your obedience to prioritize knowing God and a determination to make His will for your life your will. Success, to God, means that you are committed and intentional about displaying His character, that you value a lifestyle that is consistent with His righteousness, and that you are willing to endure whatever level of adversity necessary to honor Jesus and bring glory to His name.

Paul wrote over half of the New Testament, but he did most of it from behind prison bars. John received one of the greatest prophetic downloads from Heaven the world has ever seen, but he received it while in disgraced exile on the Island of Patmos. Stephen was a servant of servants, used by God to define the ministry of Helps for the first-generation church. Scripture describes Stephen as a man who was *"full of faith, grace, and power,"* but in the final moments of his life he was executed by stoning.

True success is not always defined by the absence of pain or attack. Sometimes the presence of attack can be an indication that you are in the will of God. As stated earlier, success is not always the accumulation of things. Whether accompanied by material possessions or not, true success is defined by a total surrender of your personal will to the will of God. It is the heart of Jesus's in prayer in the garden exclaiming, *"not my will but Thy will be done (Luke 22:42)."* True success is yielding to God's direction for your life no matter the cost. Despite Jesus' painful experience on the cross, He is the greatest expression of success the world has ever known based on His total surrender to God.

> Luke 21:1-4 NIV
> 1 As Jesus looked up, he saw the rich putting their gifts into the temple treasury. 2 He also saw a poor widow put in two very small copper coins. 3 "Truly I tell you," he said, "this poor widow has put in more than all the others. 4 All these people gave their gifts out of their wealth; but she out of her poverty put in all she had to live on."

Although abundance is clearly in the will of God for His people, it does not mean that every person that is not exhibiting overflow in their finances or perfect conditions in their life is unsuccessful.

Just because others have been graced to have greater material wealth, more well-known public platforms, or even numerically larger ministries, does not mean that they are more successful in God's eyes. *"Out of her poverty..."* the widow gave her all. When Jesus refers to this widow's lack of finances, He did not refer to it in shame due to size or amount. Her ministry did not lack substance based on the fact that it did not equate to the same material value as others who gave. It did not matter that the physical amount was less. What mattered was the value of the sacrifice. Jesus did not look at her offering as second-rate or inferior. He saw it as greater than all others due to her faithfulness to steward what she had, in the manner that God required of her. This ultimately reveals to us that Godly success is not measured in quantity, but it is measured in the quality of one's heart to honor God.

Coming out of adversity could be as simple as a shift in mindset concerning where you are. It may be as straightforward as developing an understanding, peace, and acceptance that your current condition may not be as adverse or unsuccessful as you think it is. Know that God has brought you to this place for the purpose of bringing Him the most glory, which ultimately is true success.

CHAPTER 5

Intimacy With God

Proverbs 3:1-2 NIV
1 My son, do not forget my teaching, but keep my commands in your heart, 2 for they will prolong your life many years and bring you peace and prosperity.

"Most of us are extremely effectual in our pursuit of victory. Yet, once victory has been realized, we are inconsistent in our behavior following. This routinely proves detrimental to the quest of living a victorious life. Because what you do to acquire the victory, it takes to keep the victory." – Archbishop Veron Ashe

If you would dare to be honest with yourself, during this season of seeking to come out of adversity, you probably studied more, prayed more, and even sought godly counsel more than you ever have before. Overcoming adversity usually necessitates a hunger, obedience, and commitment to God unlike any other season of your life. As a result, you have probably enjoyed a deeper level of intimacy with God as you have sought Him more. If this is true, don't let it end as you come out of negative circumstances. One destructive trait that often arises during seasons of comfort is a complacent and lackadaisical spirit. Satan frequently employs comfort to lull believers into a sense of self-sufficiency where many quickly forget God as their sustaining source in all things. Because of the grace flow that God lavishes on a person when they turn to Him, it becomes very easy to take God for granted and forget lessons learned in struggle. Unfortunately, the result is usually returning to self-destructive behavior later on.

> Exodus 20:1-6 KJV
> 1 And God spake all these words, saying, 2 I am the Lord thy God, which have brought thee out of the land of Egypt, out of the house of bondage. 3 Thou shalt have no other gods before me. 4 Thou shalt not make unto thee any graven image, or any likeness of anything that is in heaven above, or that is in the earth beneath, or that is in the water under the earth. 5 Thou shalt not bow down thyself to them, nor serve them: for I the Lord thy God am a jealous God, visiting the iniquity of the fathers upon the children unto the third and fourth generation of them that hate me; 6 And shewing mercy unto thousands of them that love me, and keep my commandments.

Many believers have issues with something I call *"Conditional Faith."* Conditional Faith is a dysfunctional mindset in which Jesus only becomes Lord of a person's life when they are being opposed or bound by negative conditions. When everything seems to be going crazy in a person's life and they are experiencing pain and discomfort, Jesus invariably becomes the center of their world in an effort to find relief. Yet, as soon as God delivers them from the hardship of their conditions, Jesus is quickly moved down on their list of importance. Jesus used to be a relationship that was prioritized, but in comfort He becomes an afterthought. If Jesus is needed, He is essential. However, the moment it is assumed that conditions are under control, the relationship with Him is put up neatly on a shelf until He is needed again.

This, in essence, is a picture of the heartbreaking cycle of sin Israel experienced throughout the Old Testament. Highlighted in the book of Judges, this pattern is a microcosm of conditional faith that conveniently demotes God on the list of priorities, based upon perceived need. Consequently, as God is removed from His position of preeminence in a person's life, grace and favor are also slowly diminished in his or her circumstances, eventually cycling one right back into other seasons of turmoil.

In this cycle there also exists an incredible revelation of God's abiding love. Despite the reality of returning struggle, God's divine nature and ultimate desire for relationship with humanity can also be clearly seen. Even when struggle is allowed, a strategic plan is simultaneously orchestrated by God to shepherd man back into intimate fellowship and favor with God. Whenever Israel sinned against God, the purpose of Him allowing their enslavement was always out of a desire to draw their hearts back to Him. The ultimate purpose of adversity is never about punishment, but it is always about relationship.

2 Corinthians 12:7-10 NIV

7...Therefore, in order to keep me from becoming conceited, I was given a thorn in my flesh, a messenger of Satan, to torment me. 8 Three times I pleaded with the Lord to take it away from me. 9 But he said to me, "My grace is sufficient for you, for my power is made perfect in weakness." Therefore I will boast all the more gladly about my weaknesses, so that Christ's power may rest on me. 10 That is why, for Christ's sake, I delight in weaknesses, in insults, in hardships, in persecutions, in difficulties. For when I am weak, then I am strong.

2 Corinthians 12 references a thorn in Paul's flesh that God refused to take away from him. Despite Paul's fervent prayer, the thorn still remained. In an earlier chapter, we learned that it is not in God's heart for any of His children to experience pain or dysfunction. Jesus died to destroy all bondage to sin and its effects.

> The ultimate purpose of adversity is never about punishment, but it is always about relationship.

However, the truth to be extracted from this passage concerns the unique ability of God to use pain to humble His children and to keep their faces turned towards Him. There is an old war adage that really drives this point home. It says, *"There are no atheists in foxholes."* When faced with great adversity, it is very difficult not to acknowledge one's need for God. Pain and adversity carry an unmatched anointing to sober you to personal inadequacies, as well as to an undeniable dependence on God's strength for deliverance. When bullets are flying all around, whether natural or spiritual, it forces every person to admit that they are helpless without God. It demands that all recognize their personal inabilities in the face of adversity and begin bowing their knees to the Lordship of Christ.

Without question, God's desire for your life is that you would live free from pain and from the assaults of the enemy. However, His greater desire is that you would live life in intimate fellowship with Him. God will often permit thorny circumstances in your life to preserve a level of closeness with you that would not exist otherwise. The enemy purposes adversity as a means of attack, but God purposes adversity as a prelude to His revealed grace and an invitation to intimate fellowship.

> James 4:10 KJV
> 10 Humble yourselves in the sight of the Lord, and he shall lift you up.

When you really look at adversity, each instance is an open appeal by God for you to take a posture of humility and submission. It is a faith test for you to remain consistent in His character, with an expectation of His divine uplifting.

Defining Intimacy

Intimacy with God is a pursuit of Him without carnal agenda. It is a desire for God's presence above any need for Him to do anything outside of what He has already done. More than something to obtain, intimacy is an intentionality to abide in Him as He abides in you. It is living a life in which every movement, every thought, every experience is driven by a full dependence on and a life-sustaining passion for His tangible presence. It is a quest to know God, to look into His eyes with no other motive but to share in the testimony that angels have exclaimed since the beginning of time, *"Holy!"*

Intimacy is the posture of your heart towards God when everything revolves around an unquenchable fire to know and honor Him. It is a life lived beyond striving, and a life fully aware of God each and every step of the way. Intimacy is your personal acknowledgment of Jesus as Emmanuel, God with you at all times, in every moment, and in every circumstance. Like the child who refrains from bad behavior when their parents are around, living fully aware of God's tangible presence empowers you to live uprightly before Him as well. Like Abram in Genesis 17:1, intimacy is an acceptance of a divine calling to walk before God and to be blameless.

> Psalm 27:4 KJV
> 4 One thing have I desired of the Lord, that will I seek after; that I may dwell in the house of the Lord all the days of my life, to behold the beauty of the Lord, and to enquire in his temple.

David's one desire in life was to *dwell* with God. To dwell means to remain. It also means to inhabit or to marry. Intimacy is a determination to live in complete consciousness of God's presence. It is a covenant marriage of your spirit with His Spirit, in which submitted obedience becomes the identifying wedding band that you choose to wear. With the same effort a wife seeks to share life in oneness with her husband, intimacy is a personal pursuit of oneness with Jesus.

As with any marriage, intimacy does not mean that supernatural manifestations of God's power will always be present. Every day may not be as celebratory as the wedding itself, but due to the covenant bond you share with God, you should always endeavor to honor the marriage by living aware of His abiding presence in everything you say and do.

> It is a covenant marriage of your spirit with His Spirit, in which submitted obedience becomes the identifying wedding band that you choose to wear.

Galatians 5:16-17 & 22-25 KJV
16 But I say, walk by the Spirit, and you will not gratify the desires of the flesh. 17 For the desires of the flesh are against the Spirit, and the desires of the Spirit are against the flesh, for these are opposed to each other, to keep you from doing the things you want to do.

22 But the fruit of the Spirit is love, joy, peace, patience, kindness, goodness, faithfulness, 23 gentleness, self-control; against such things there is no law. 24 And those who belong to Christ Jesus have crucified the flesh with its passions and desires. 25 If we live by the Spirit, let us also keep in step with the Spirit.

Intimacy with God isn't being extreme, over-spiritual, or legalistic. Legalism is an attempt to win God's approval through doing. Intimacy, however, is a Spirit-led walk of abiding and living from an understanding that you are already approved by God and made right through faith in Jesus Christ. It's from this understanding that you are empowered to live lives of supernatural obedience in step with God's Spirit.

Fully embracing God's covenant presence and living from relationship enables you to just be. The same Holy Spirit that exists in Jesus also lives in those who accept Him. Whenever you place your faith in Jesus and choose to live aware of Him, you are given supernatural authority to say *NO* to selfish carnality and to produce fruit that reveals Christ's divine nature. The more you gaze into the eyes of Jesus through intimacy, in time you naturally become like Him *(1 John 3:2)*. Intimacy with God is powerful because intimacy is the supernatural environment of transformation.

> Exodus 33:7-11 NIV
> 7 Now Moses used to take a tent and pitch it outside the camp some distance away, calling it the "tent of meeting." Anyone inquiring of the Lord would go to the tent of meeting outside the camp. 8 And whenever Moses went out to the tent, all the people rose and stood at the entrances to their tents, watching Moses until he entered the tent. 9 As Moses went into the tent, the pillar of cloud would come down and stay at the entrance, while the Lord spoke with Moses. 10 Whenever the people saw the pillar of cloud standing at the entrance to the tent, they all stood and worshiped, each at the entrance to their

tent. 11 The Lord would speak to Moses face to face, as one speaks to a friend. Then Moses would return to the camp, but his young aide Joshua, son of Nun, did not leave the tent.

Joshua 1:5 KJV
1 "As I was with Moses; so I will be with thee. I will not fail thee, nor forsake thee."

When Moses died, Joshua assumed leadership of Israel with an assurance of God's commitment to walk with him in the same manner He had walked with Moses. To the degree Joshua witnessed God for years guiding his mentor Moses, Joshua was now being told by God to enter into an equivalent level of intimacy. The only key was discerning how to access it.

So, how did Moses acquire intimacy with God? The answer derives from Moses' complete dependency on God and his concerted efforts to pursue Him. The relationship Moses experienced with God was no ordinary relationship. Their bond was distinguished by the unparalleled frequency with which Moses retreated into God's presence. He routinely took journeys outside of the hustle and bustle of everyday life to pursue God in the Tent of Meetings. Due to Moses establishing this pattern of pursuit, God purposefully honored Moses's intentionality by descending in the form of a cloud to speak to him *"face to face as friend."* This offers a powerful illustration for every person seeking to grow in their intimate relationship with God. Moses prioritized God, so God prioritized Moses by showing up. When you seek God, you find Him. When you draw near to God, He draws near to you. When you avail yourself to God, He is faithful to open Himself to you. God is not a respecter of persons *(Acts 10:34)*, but He is a respecter of faith. Just as Moses accessed God's intimate presence through prioritization, so can you. Developing a habit of putting God first by carving out both time and space not only worked for Moses, it will, without question, work for you. Setting aside a specific time and location is not only a practice that can be seen in the life of Moses, it can also be seen in the life of Jesus. From being a child in the temple courts of Jerusalem, to praying all night alone before preaching the Sermon on the Mount, to even a moment of intense travail in the garden of Gethsemane before the cross, Jesus' life was defined by His practice of prioritizing intimacy with God.

>Proverbs 29:18 KJV
>18 Where there is no vision, the people perish: but he that keepeth the law, happy is he.

Prioritizing God has to become more than just lip service or a good idea. It has to be deliberately planned and practiced before it will ever produce tangible fruit. Without a vision, an intentional plan, you will never walk in the intimacy that God intends for you. Remember, *"He that keeps the law will be happy."* The word law in this passage not only refers to Biblical instructions, it also refers to a consistent decision to walk out God's established customs of behavior. It is a disciplined lifestyle that is motivated by maintaining God's holy standard. Intimacy with God is a purposed commitment to actively value and honor your relationship with Him.

So, what does carving out time and space look like? What does prioritizing God really mean? The following are two examples that I hope will help you better understand this concept.

Intimacy: Your Spiritual GPS

Every time we get in the car, despite a working knowledge of where we may be going, my wife takes out her phone and checks the map app for the best directions for our trip. No matter the distance to be traveled or whether we have already taken a particular route a hundred times before, the question invariably comes, *"Do you need me to check the route?"* Even to the extent of us going to work at the church, roads that we have traveled pretty much every day for years, my wife still pulls out her phone to determine the quickest route for us to take. Being your typical male, this practice used to always frustrate me. Seeing her pull out that phone, and hearing her ask that question, disturbed every ounce of testosterone and ego I possessed. It would sometimes frustrate me so severely that I would actually ask her to turn down the volume on her phone so that I would not be annoyed by an inanimate voice sharing directions that I already knew. This frustration persisted for some time, until recently. I was traveling to work alone when my eyes were opened to the importance of my wife's routine. On this particular day, no app was pulled up and no directions were sought. Life was good, so I thought. Then traffic hit.

To my unfortunate amazement, I soon discovered that construction was causing heavy backup along most of the way that I normally traveled. In addition to the construction, there was a wreck about half-way to work that slowed traffic even more. A commute that generally took me 45 minutes to navigate, on this particular day, took me over two-and-a-half hours. When I look back on this moment, I can't help but acknowledge the difference a simple practice of checking an app would have made had I only taken the time to do so. Had I checked, the app would have revealed every road construction, accident, and any other obstacle that I was due to encounter. If I had simply checked, the app would have not only alerted me to the obstacles along my route, it would have also offered alternate routes that would have enabled me to avoid unnecessary trouble and would have gotten me to my destination in a more efficient, less stressful way. Had I only slowed down and taken some time, I would have undoubtedly saved some time.

Intimacy with God is the same. Creating time and space to commune with God is a practice that provides clear directions for where you are going. Intimacy with God is a routine of making the normal demands of life less urgent, while at the same time raising God in your consciousness and purposely prioritizing Him over everything else. It is a determination to live life at a reduced pace in which the journey with God is more important than the destination He is taking you to.

> Intimacy is a determination to live life at a reduced pace in which the journey with God is more important than the destination He is taking you to.

It is the acknowledgment of Him in all things before you decide to make a move. Whether God changes your direction or confirms that you are on the right path, intimacy is the consistent intentionality to give Him the opportunity to alert you to the obstacles and obstructions that may lay ahead through study, prayer, worship, and meditation. It is developing a routine of interacting with His presence that supersedes all other relationships and is the primary compass for every step that you take. Creating time and space is a commitment to regularly take daily sabbaticals, retreating into God's presence, and searching for His voice, as you trust Him to reroute your path around demonic spiritual traffic in everyday life.

Intimacy: Your Field of Dreams

I am reminded of an old 1989 film classic, *"Field of Dreams."* In this movie, a struggling Iowa farmer, Ray Kinsella, as he is walking through his cornfields, hears a mysterious voice repeating the phrase, *"If you build it, they will come!"* Led by this voice, Ray is compelled to ignore conventional wisdom, abandon the norms of traditional farming, and initiate a plan to build a full-sized baseball diamond in a major section of his fields. Ray's desire was to know the voice that called him over the potential consequences of his personal sacrifice. He invested all he had in an effort to be obedient to the unfamiliar. Upon completion of the baseball diamond, to his wonderment and great joy, ghosts of legendary baseball players of the past begin to emerge from the surrounding cornfields with a longing desire to play on the field that Ray had built. Through what he sacrificed, Ray was rewarded with supernatural relationships that transformed his life and that of his family in every way. He built it, and the supernatural emerged.

Similarly, the voice of God calls us into intimacy with Him. Like Ray in his cornfields, or Moses in the Tent of Meetings, intimacy is a purposed plan to set a regular appointment with God. It is a calculated and intentional sacrifice of what is normal in an effort to possess a greater supernatural presence. Carving out time and space is an actual entry on your daily calendar that is labeled *"God's Time."* It is a commitment to a fellowship with God that supersedes every other appointment and task. It is a joyful communion in which the reward is less about the results that come from doing and more about the relationship that comes from just being. Like Ray's experience, intimacy is less about an ability to play, and more about The ONE who comes to dwell with you on the field you build. Whether it is a room or closet, a park bench, or an office, if you build it, God will come.

> Revelation 3:20 NIV
> 20 Here I am! I stand at the door and knock. If anyone hears my voice and opens the door, I will come in and eat with that person, and they with me.

What place have you dedicated as your field of dreams with God? Where is the place in your life that God knows when you go there you are fully invested in hearing, seeing, and obeying Him? What routine have you set in place that says to God, "This time belongs to You Lord, and You alone?" What do you sacrifice daily to experience God's divine fellowship and GPS in your life? I ask all these questions, not as a form of judgment, but rather as an indicator to determine how committed you are to enjoying intimacy with God. God wants a relationship with you, but He always desires an open invitation. He wants to know that you prioritize Him. He wants to know that His presence trumps everything else in your life. Carving out time and space for God opens the door of your heart and welcomes Him to fellowship with you. This is not an act of self-righteousness or to complete a spiritual checklist. It is an effort to build strong biblical practices that keep you fully connected to His divine presence. The sacrifice you make to build these spiritual practices and habits should never be a quest for material gain or even carnal favor. This should always be a quest for God Himself. Your sacrifice should never be a desire for the residue that comes after you exit the tent. Your sacrifice should always be about the descending cloud that chooses to show up at the designated time you go in. The corn that you give up in pursuit of God is far less valuable or important than the relationship that emerges. Your time away from the camp of life is a small price to pay for the glory that is committed to meeting you. Build it, and He will come!

For Moses, intimacy with God was not the source of his reward. It was his reward. God's presence was so vital to Moses that He refused to take hold of the Promised Land without God's commitment to be with them when they possessed it (Exodus 33:15). Likewise, true intimacy with God means that you always desire The Blesser far more than you desire the blessing.

If you take anything away from this book, please understand that ***intimacy with God is the key to your victory in every season of adversity.*** Every victory you will ever experience, you will do so by God's grace, not your own power. Make a practice of pursuing God with all your heart, soul, and mind. Make His will your life's pursuit and His fellowship your passion.

Create an atmosphere around your life that is driven by a constant desire to hear God, believe God, and obey God. Choose to abide under the shadow of His fellowship as you live fully aware of His abiding presence. Remain consistent in your pursuit of God, so that you will continue to experience His manifested presence

> Intimacy with God is the key to your victory in every season of adversity.

in your life. The greatest deterrent to prolonged seasons of adversity is total submission to God's will through an intentional love pursuit of Him. Make God your prize. Submit all that you are to Him. In all your ways acknowledge the Lord and watch as He directs your path out of adversity into a glorious land of promise and His divine presence.

FINAL WORD

Enjoy The Journey

> Psalm 16:11 NIV
> 11 You make known to me the path of life; you will fill me with joy in your presence, with eternal pleasures at your right hand.

NO MATTER WHERE YOU find yourself in life, God has a plan and a willingness to bring you victoriously through adversity. No matter how difficult your circumstances, God has destined for you to overcome. You simply need to trust Him to get through every moment. God's love for you reaches further than the natural mind can conceive. He loves you so dearly that even before you ever chose Him, He made provision for you to be accepted through the death, burial, and resurrection of His Son, Jesus Christ. By giving Jesus to die for your sins, God made an open confession of His unequaled love and of the eternal value you hold in His heart. If He loved you enough to give you Jesus, how much more is He willing to give you deliverance and freedom!

Be encouraged that you are closer to breakthrough than you have ever been before. Stand firm in your faith with a confident expectation of your coming victory. God is a God of limitless possibilities. Despite any difficulty you face, know that there is nothing too hard for God. He is both fully capable and fully willing to manifest His goodness in your life, in all situations. You need only to repent, change destructive behavior, learn the lessons God assigns, submit to His will in every area, stay consistent in pursuit of Him through the good and the bad, and then watch from a seat of intimacy as God continues to manifest His victory in your life for His glory.

Enjoy the journey!

ABOUT THE AUTHOR
Todd Holts

Declaring a message of hope, centered on the unconditional redemptive love of God through faith in Jesus, Todd Holts is a passionate teacher, preacher, and communicator of the Gospel. He has an extraordinary gift for inspiring people of all ages and walks of life, to become all that God has called them to be through a life of love and service.

As an ordained minister for over 25 years, Todd has served Christ's Kingdom in a variety of ways, ranging from custodian to senior pastor. He met and married his wife, Tanya, while serving as Youth Pastor of St. John's UMC. They are the proud parents of three: Tyrah, Tohnnia, and Christian.

Todd currently serves on the pastoral staff of Get Wrapped Church in Spring, Texas, under the leadership of Pastor Juan Martinez.

Connect With Me!

toddholts.com

Want to write a book but don't know where to start?

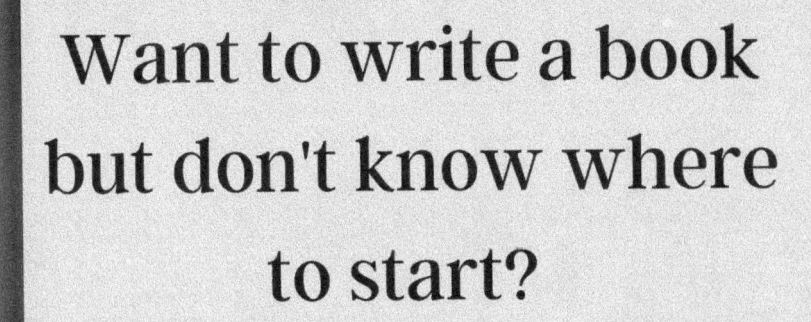

Contact Greatness Makers Today!

Making you great is our business.

Printed in the USA
CPSIA information can be obtained
at www.ICGtesting.com
CBHW051718101023
1296CB00005B/94